# THE LOVE
# SONGS OF SAPPHO

# THE LOVE
# SONGS OF SAPPHO

*Translated with an Essay by Paul Roche*
*Introduction by Page duBois*

LITERARY CLASSICS

 **Prometheus Books**

59 John Glenn Drive
Amherst, New York 14228-2197

Published 1998 by Prometheus Books

02  01          5  4  3  2

Library of Congress Cataloging-in-Publication Data

Sappho.
   [Works. English. 1998]
   The love songs of Sappho / translated with an essay by Paul
Roche ; introduction by Page duBois.
     p.   cm. — (Literary classics)
   Includes bibliographical references.
   ISBN 1–57392–251–X (alk. paper)
   1. Sappho—Translations into English. 2. Love poetry, Greek—
Translations into English. 3. Women—Greece—Poetry. I. Roche,
Paul, 1927–   . II. Title. III. Series: Literary classics (Amherst,
N.Y.)
PA4408.E5R63   1998
884′.01—dc21
                                      98–38950
                                         CIP

Printed in the United States of America on acid-free paper

For Erica, my first grandchild,
in memory of another Erica,
my first publisher*

ἔγω δὲ φιλημ' ἀβροσύναν, κέκλυτε τοῦτο, κάι μοι
τὸ λάμπρον ἔρος τὠελίω καὶ τὸ κάλον λέλογχε

(Sappho—edm.II8a)

As for me—listen well—
my delight is the exquisite;
yes, for me glitter and sunlight and love
are one society.

*Erica Marx: *The Rat and the Convent Dove,* Hand & Flower
Press, 1952.

ΠΟΙΚΙΛΟΘΡΟΝΑΘΑΝΑΤΑΦΡΟΔΙΤΑ
ΠΑΙΔΙΟΣΔΟΛΟΠΛΟΚΕΛΙΣΣΟΜΑΙΣΕ
ΜΗΜΑΣΑΙΣΙΜΗΔΟΝΙΑΙΣΙΔΑΜΝΑ
ΠΟΤΝΙΑΘΥΜΟΝ
ΑΛΛΑΤΥΔΕΑΘΑΙΠΟΤΑΚΑΤΕΡΩΤΑ
ΤΑΣΕΜΑΣΑΥΔΑΣΑΟΙΣΑΠΗΛΟΙ
ΕΚΛΥΕΣΠΑΤΡΟSΔΕΔΟΜΟΝΛΙΠΟΙΣΑ
ΧΡΥΣΙΟΝΗΛΘΕS

If there existed a papyrus, vellum, or wax tablet dating from Sappho's time, it would look very much like the above (the first two verses of Sappho's most famous and her only complete poem, the *Call to Aphrodite, No. 17*).

# ACKNOWLEDGMENTS

I owe continued gratitude to the late Donald W. Lucas, Percival Maitland Laurence Reader in Classics in the University of Cambridge and Fellow of King's College, Cambridge, who corrected and steadied my first efforts to put together a portrait of Sappho in 1961.

Present gratitude to Dr. Rowland Smith of Trinity College, Oxford, who has saved me from several pitfalls.

I am indebted, too, to Pat Gilbert-Read and to my editors at New American Library, Hugh Rawson, Susan Rogers, and Rosemary Ahern for making valuable suggestions to improve my original Introduction, now entitled "Portrait of Sappho."

# Introduction

THE ANCIENT Greek poet Sappho writes of Aphrodite the goddess of sexuality, of soft beds, roses, groves sacred to the goddess, of jealousy, desire, and the absence of one's beloved. Setting themselves against the warrior culture of Homer, against the values of labor and reproduction emerging in the nascent city-states of the Greek world, Sappho's fragmentary, broken lines celebrate pleasure and women's bodies. We have come to recognize that the classical tradition, long privileged as the source of all that is most unique about the Eurocentric past, is just one of many traditions informing our postmodern, multi-ethnic reality. Even within the Greco-Roman tradition, however, there are voices that survive in opposition within a seemingly univocal culture. Sappho, the only woman whose poetry has come down to us from antiquity, sings not of work and war, not of the instrumentalizing of the body, but of the individual and her subjective body, of "the most beautiful," of erotic desire of yearning.

Sappho was born in the seventh century before the common era (B.C.E.) on the island of Lesbos. We know her work only in fragments. Although other authors in antiquity report the existence of volumes of Sappho's works, we have only ruins, lines cited in these later authors' work, lines painstakingly reconstructed from ancient papyruses exhumed from Egyptian sands. Many have attempted to construct biographies on these magnificent ruins, to invent reassuring narratives of teaching, motherhood, heterosexuality. But such narratives are based on nothing, on accounts of poets and writers who wrote hundreds of years after

Sappho's death. Still there remains much that could be said, tracing the nature of Sappho's work, its influence on the poets who followed her, the mythologizing of Sappho's life, the transmission of her works, their unhappy fate at the hands of copiers and the accidents of centuries that separate her from us. I want here rather to concentrate on just two issues: the relation of Sappho as a poet to the poetic and cultural context in which she found herself, and the issues of sexuality that Sappho's work excites for many readers.

Sappho writes in the seventh century B.C.E., after the great age of Minoan culture, after the immigration of Greek speakers into the Mediterranean basin, after the period of Mycenaean domination over Crete and much of mainland Greece, after the fall of Mycenae, after the dark age which followed it, and after the time of Homer. Hers was an age of earliest literacy, of an Aegean recently transformed from a devastated region in which the residents had lost the capacity to write, had lost all the great organization and hierarchical structure of a warrior and palace culture. As the Greek world began to recover from the terrible effects of a mysterious catastrophe of the twelfth century B.C.E., cities emerged from the ruins of the past and in the regions of the Aegean world to which its refugees had fled. Homer the great poet, the first poet of the Western tradition whose work has come down to us, is now believed to have written or sung his epic poems in the eighth century B.C.E.; he was probably a privileged singer, one who served princes, who sang in great houses not unlike those of the Homeric heroes. The world of Sappho, at least a century later, was a very different one, one that valued urbanity as much as militarism. In her day the cities of the Eastern Aegean had become centers of culture and of luxury; just such a city, Mytilene, close to Asia Minor, to the wealth and cultivation of the Persians, harbored not only a surplus that allowed for the development of urban life; it also permitted the aristocracy to which Sappho belonged a life of leisure and high culture.

Sappho writes, I believe, in full consciousness of her

status as an aristocrat, and of her place as a woman aristocrat whose poetic context is formed by men poets' epic celebration of war and warrior culture. Along with such figures as Arkhilokhos, she is part of a great turn in the poetic tradition, and in the very history of the development of subjectivity. Homer and Hesiod, her predecessors in the epic age, speak of themselves not as individual men, but as conduits of divine inspiration, as transmitters of truth and lies, of stories and genealogies, of histories that the gods and muses know, which they convey to the mouths of the poets. Sappho and the poets who are her near contemporaries are the first to speak in the first-person singular, to use the word "I" to anchor their poetic speech, to hollow out for their listeners and readers the cultural space for a creating subjectivity. For us the existence of a self with interiority, with a silent, private consciousness, harboring secrets of fantasy, imagination, sexuality, may seem perfectly inevitable. But this, like other assumptions of twentieth-century culture, is a construction, the result of a centuries-long process, of many transformations, accretions, and losses. We see in the work of Sappho the very beginnings of this process, the construction of selfhood, of the fiction of subjectivity, at its origins. The community of Homeric heroes, of men feasting around a camp fire, dividing up the spoils of battle—spoils which included the women of the conquered people—conceived of identity as collective; the hero's selfhood was diffusely connected with his tribe, with the name of his father, with the legacy of heroic actions his name would carry in the memory of the future. It is only in the age of the burgeoning city, of a newly emerging possibility of democracy, of popular agitation against traditional aristocratic rule, that noble birth and blood begin to become less important than individual citizens' separate status and identities, identities that will become putatively equal and interchangeable in the radical democracy of fifth-century Athens.

Sappho is a crucial figure in this process of separating out individuality from the communal mass of pre-urban society. Her poetic representations of desire and subjectivity, of an "I" that sings and wills, that suffers jealousy and longing, begin to open up a space for private, interior life, a life that will not be realized for centuries to come. Her poetic project seems to include the establishing of this sort of identity, a figuring of human energy that now seems commonplace to us, but that was once an astonishing social and intellectual phenomenon in a world in which the heroic family had long been the only matrix within which significant life could be lived and represented in verse.

Sappho's poems intervene in the heroic tradition in a variety of ways. The poem here numbered 55, "A cavalry corps, a column of men. . . ." exhibits one dimension of Sappho's striking position in the history of Western culture. This poem uses the world of war, of infantry, cavalry, and fleets, as a background against which a proto-philosophical question is set. The problem is that of abstraction. How does one generate a universal category from the ephemera of life, of individuals' desires, how does the general emerge from the particular? Abstract thinking here constructs a logically higher category, one that asserts not only that Helen was beautiful, but that also seeks to find what Helen shares with other beautiful things as it asks: "what is the most beautiful?" Sappho poses a question with great intellectual sophistication. When she answers this question, it is not simply with a claim about her lover, a boast that might lead to a verbal duel like those physical struggles of the Homeric heroes, who ask again and again the question, "who is the greatest warrior?" and then proceed to combat, arguing the case with their armored bodies. This poem asks, "what is the most beautiful?" and then answers this question with a definition. This is a solution inconceivable to Homer; his is a world of particular heroes, of past generations, of fathers and sons and the long-delayed pleasures of homecoming. Sappho rather, in a move that seems at first to proceed contradictorily against the projection of a new individualism, a private subjectivity, is caught up not in a private response, but in a general meditation, an answer to the question that satisfies all human beings: The most beautiful thing is ὅττω τις ἔροται, which I would translate as "what one loves."

One might imagine that Sappho's new capacity to reason abstractly, like the emergence of the subjective I, is possible only in this particular moment in history. This possibility of generalization, of thinking categorically, is part of a greater transformation of ancient culture. The invention of coined money occurred in proximity to Sappho's native island city of Mitylene, in nearby Lydia, in the seventh century B.C.E.; this event marked a major alteration in social and economic relations in the West. The notion that a coin, a piece of money, can be thought of as abstractly equivalent both to a roll of linen cloth and to a pair of amphorae filled with wine, requires an abstraction of what these things share, what their common "exchange" value might be. Such a conceptualization of value is highly pertinent to a poem about "the most beautiful thing." A creature of her world, a rapidly altering universe of new cities, new sources of wealth in which value inheres not only in land, the traditional possession of aristocrats and of founding citizens, but also in goods, in manufactured and traded objects, Sappho makes a move of first philosophy, seeking to define, in a project that will later be taken up by Plato and Aristotle, a higher order of things.

In this poem Sappho returns, after citing the experience of the most beautiful woman, Helen, who follows her desire and leaves her family to be with her lover, to the woman whom Sappho herself loves. But her account of Anaktoria is significantly different from the descriptions of desire in her contemporaries' erotic poetry, in that she returns to her own desire as it is subsumed under the general category of "what one loves," itself an exposition of the category "the most beautiful." Thus her love becomes a particular example of a general case rather than a purely private meditation on the question. Here the individual's experience becomes comprehensible as example, rather than as one temporal moment in a heroic history, in the evolution of a great family. It may be that the individualism we see in Sappho's work, the introduction of an intensely realized first-person singular, is possible only when generality is theorizable, when the possibility of a higher logical order is also assumed.

The great brilliance of Sappho's poetry consists not only in her representation of a new stage in the thinking of existence, of the place of the inidividual and her desire, not only in her evocation of pleasure, luxury, and meditation on loss; it is also a superb example of turning preexisting poetic materials to a new use, to a poetic project different from that for which they were first composed. Helen, an ambiguous object of exchange in Homer's hands, becomes an agent of desire in Sappho's. Sappho also refigures Homer's poetic formulation of flight and pursuit. Warriors pursue each other in elegant patterns of variation throughout the Homeric corpus. Man ambushes man, chases him through the ranks of warriors and chariots, around trees, around the city wall of Troy, engages in the endless pursuit and flight of single combat. Sappho takes a crucial motif of the battlefield, this situation which epitomizes enmity, the establishing of hierarchy that is martial domination, and uses it to speak of love. The poem here numbered 17, *Call to Aphrodite*, works on the play between the roles of pursuer and pursued so crucial on the battlefield. Here Aphrodite is invoked, begged to come down to earth, to the narrator's side, as she has come in the past, to promise to transform the girl who now flees into the one who pursues, the one who receives gifts into the one who offers them. The reversibility of these roles, the tricks of fortune in love that make one the lover, the other the beloved, are playfully yet hauntingly represented here. The voice of Sappho supplicates the female god to intervene in a scene of pursuit and flight between two women; Sappho reinscribes her probable source, Homer's *Iliad*, making hers a poem of homoerotic courtship. This is not to say that Sappho is gentle and feminine and desires to subvert the violence and enmity of the masculine war machine. In fact, like other archaic lyric poets, she seems to have seen love as a battlefield, the terrain of erotic struggle one of victory and loss, of pain as well as ecstasy.

An implicit narrative of loss and a concomitant yearning drives Sappho's poetics, but unlike Homeric poetics, which invoke a historically distant and irrecoverable age of heroism, Sappho's often conjure up past or future pleasure, addressing an imagined lover who remains absent, who comes to life only through words. Although there are many poems so fragmentary that we cannot deduce their themes, others that celebrate weddings or other occasions, in the most complete extant poems the voice of the narrator again and again describes a distant, unattainable object of desire. This patern is characteristic of such poems as the invocation of the distant Aphrodite in poem 17, the Anaktoria poem (55), recalling Anaktoria "not present," the poem for Atthis (53), mourning the girl now far away in Lydia. In many poems we find a relationship between desire and withholding, or presence and absence, which seems to move Sappho to write, to create in the elusive, illusive word the absent one, the desired one. In poem 92, which some scholars believe not to be Sappho's work, made up of two disparate fragments which describe an apple left high on a tree, a flower trampled underfoot, metaphors often used of maidens, Sappho's lines enact the drama of desire and withholding, presence and absensc: "Like the last red apple/ sweet and high . . ." The apple here is unattainable, high on its branch; the simile makes the apple present even as it records its distance, its hauteur. Like the gatherers, the reader recognizes the beauty of the fruit but cannot ever reach it. This fragment typifies Sapphic poetics and allows us to thematize the act of reading itself as a recording of the experience of absence, the process of seeing and not seeing simultaneously. We can know the apple only through the poem, but the poem cannot be the apple, can only realize for us its unattainability. The reader assumes the position of the thwarted gatherers, of the assumed suitors, of the poet; the act of reading is an attempt to constitute the missing fruit, the missing maiden, to bring them to life in words that must always betray the materiality of the real. These songs must be contrasted with the conventional themes of Greek poetry, especially in later Greek tragedy, describing women as objects of exchange, as fields to be plowed, tablets to be inscribed. In the Sappho fragments women are the signifiers of potential significance in an otherwise ephemeral world.

Although we know almost nothing about the performance of Sappho's poems, about the immediate environment of her production of them, it is clear from the language she uses that she writes as a woman "narrator," in a feminine voice, desiring other women. For twentieth-century readers of her verse, this dimension of her work offers a continuity with contemporary Lesbian practices. It also transforms our view of classical antiquity as an exclusively male-dominated society, one in which women had no voice. And Sappho's poems present a powerful challenge to what has often been seen as a monolithically phallic economy, an untroubled history of heterosexuality triumphant through all of Western culture. Sappho celebrates not household labor and fertility, not the role of the good wife but rather desire and yearning, the amorous pleasures women share on soft beds; in poem 54 the narrator remembers: "All the garlands woven/Around your delicate neck,/Fashioned from a hundred flowers./All the fragrance of myrrh/Fit for a queen and rare/Worn on your fresh young skin beside me,/While on the softest beds/From the quiet hands of maids/No Ionian was so feted." Sappho sings again and again of her love and desire for women.

This latter fact of Sappho's poetic corpus has led to immense difficulties in the transmission and appreciation of her work. Although the poets and thinkers of Greek antiquity seem to have had no problems with Sappho's clearly articulated desire for women, scandalized Christians of subsequent generations and the scholars of classical antiquity of the early modern and modern eras have spent much ink on the question of Sapphic desire. Some have claimed that Sappho "ventriloquates" male desire, that she speaks for men in singing of the love for women. Some have argued that she participates in a genre peculiar to archaic poetry, in which adolescent girls desired each other in preparation for lives of heterosexuality and reproduction. Others have fantasized that Sappho was a schoolmistress, a poet who trained girls in the arts of the muses, sent them away, and yearned for them forever after. Editors and translators have tried to erase, correct, ignore the clear textual traces of Lesbian desire in Sappho's poetry. Recently, however, political struggles for gay and Lesbian rights, and work in the history of sexuality have enabled a less biased reading of Greek culture, allowing us to escape, condemn, and even to historicize the anachronistic homophobia of much of the Judaeo-Christian tradition in its attitudes toward classical antiquity.

Michel Foucault and others have argued, for example, that the social role of "homosexual" is really a construction of recent centuries, that the cultural demand that individuals choose a sexual identity and name themselves according to their object of desire is a product of a particular, late moment in human history. The sexual practices of the ancient Greeks have been especially interesting to historians of sexuality, particularly because of what seems to be a unique institution in Western culture, the open and often celebrated practice of pederasty, eros between young men and boys, in the classical city. It has been argued recently that sexual identity was constructed in classical culture not on the basis of the gender of one's sexual partner, but rather on one's position in sexual acts, as active or passive, dominating or receiving, penetrating or penetrated. Sexual practices were thought of in terms of power—power over others, control over oneself. The male Greek citizen was the subject of domination and desire; women, slaves, and boys were his objects. Such an argument sheds light on our difference from the ancient Greeks, and supports the view that sexual identity, like other features of human society, varies historically, that identities are constructed differently in different social and economic circumstances. With such an interpretation of the changing forms that identity takes in human history, we can no longer rely on common sense, on our mistaken ideas about so-called "human nature," to explain away cultural differences in the domain of sexuality.

There is little said of women's desire for women in the classical age; Plato in the dialogue called the *Symposium* has his character Aristophanes speak of prehistoric creatures composed of male/male, male/female, and female/female halves, to account for what we now call Lesbian desire. But we are forced to conclude from the paucity of evidence concerning women's sexuality either that there was no Lesbian practice in antiquity after Sappho (highly unlikely), or that it was so tabooed a subject that it could not be alluded to (also unlikely given that Aristophanes, for example, speaks of a great variety of sexual practices with great relish), or that it was taken for granted and considered insignificant, like many other aspects of women's lives. The latter explanation seems to me most likely. If what were thought of as sexual practices characteristically involved penetration, the continuum of Lesbian practices may not even have seemed like "sexual" acts in the eyes of the Greeks. In what we might see as a range of sexual behaviors, performed from adolescence to old age, with most women marrying and having children, with various modes of sexual expression, woman-woman sex, leading neither to the breaking of the hymen and therefore to the loss of highly prized virginity, nor to reproduction, may have seemed irrelevant to the men of the classical city, engaged as they were in such weighty matters as politics, the maintenance of honor, and the seduction of boys. Women, on the other hand, may have taken pleasure with each other, as they did in Sappho's day, without a poet by to record their desire.

Suggestive as it is, the new work on sexuality, with some major exceptions, focuses primarily on men. It is not clear, for example, how Foucault's formulations about sexuality would affect our understanding of Sappho. She sings of weddings, of a daughter, and of desire for women. Can we conclude then, that the desire for women was part of a rich and varied sexual existence for women of her class, that they, like male aristocrats, could conduct an erotic life that included as objects of desire both males and females? Or does the form that the erotic takes in her poetry, her emphasis on her desire for women, contradict the thesis that the gender of one's sexual partner was irrelevant to the ancient Greeks? These are subjects for future studies that do not make the existence of women a footnote to the history of men. In any case, although Sappho's Lesbian desire has proven intolerable to generations of male classical scholars, it never affected her high reputation as a poet in antiquity. We must conclude that her expressions of love for women were completely acceptable to her readers in ancient Greece, since they excite no comment, neither praise nor blame.

In raising such issues as the open celebration of women's desire for women, Sappho's poems help us to understand the importance of the study of classical antiquity in our present day, one in which we are caught up gazing at a future without history. We encounter in the culture of the ancient Greeks not only a culture named as the origin of our own. We also must come to terms with its otherness, with constructions of identity, sexuality, and society that differ radically from our own and reveal the arbitrary nature of arrangements we take for granted in our society of compulsory heterosexuality, egoism, and consumerism.

Sappho's poem 53 exemplifies some of the wonders of her poetics. This poem transforms inherited material of ancient culture, in particular the theme of the woman's body as a field to be plowed by her husband, a field in which his planted seed will grow and be harvested as a crop of new male citizens for the city. It speaks of loss, of the absent beloved one, now far away in Lydia, the site of Asiatic luxury, and the invention of coined money. It recalls to life a woman now lost to the narrator and makes the loss of her the occasion of poetry: "Now far above the ladies of Lydia, /Like a moon at sunset rising dewy-/Fingered among the stars and/Shedding her light on the salty sea/And over the flowery fields where the lovely/Dewdrops lie and the roses/Rear and the lacy chervil blooms with the/Melilot, so she wanders remembering. . . ." Sappho's poem, set under the sign of the moon, a goddess, rather than under the light of Helios, the sun god, celebrates not labor, the nourishing crops of grain, productive of wealth, of new sons for the city, its sustenance, but rather flowers, pleasure for its own sake—roses and thyme and "sweet-blooming honey-lotus." This great poet, lover of women, shines like a moon over Western culture; she is the lost one herself, shining in the darkness, speaking of desire for the same, speaking of difference.

—Page duBois

# SUGGESTIONS FOR FURTHER READING

Dover, J.K. *Greek Homosexuality*. Cambridge, Mass.: 1978.

duBois, Page. *Sowing the Body: Psychoanalysis and Ancient Representations of Women*. Chicago: 1988.

———. "Sappho and Helen." In *Women in the Ancient World: The Arethusa Papers*, ed. John Peradotto and J.P. Sullivan. Albany, New York: 1984, 95–105.

Foucault, Michel. *The Use of Pleasure*, trans. R. Hurley. New York: 1985.

Gans, Eric, "Naissance du moi lyrique: Du feminin au masculin." *Poétique* 46 (1981), 129–39.

Hallett, Judith. "Sappho and Her Social Context: Sense and Sensuality." *Signs* 4 (Spring 1979): 447–64.

Halperin, David. *One Hundred Years of Homosexuality*. New York: 1990.

Lefkowitz, Mary. *The Lives of the Ancient Poets*. Baltimore: 1981.

McEvilley, T. "Sappho, Fragment Two." *Phoenix* 26 (1972): 323–33.

Page, Denys. *Sappho and Alcaeus*. Oxford: 1955.

Stigers, Eva Stehle. "Sappho's Private World." In *Reflections of Women in Antiquity*. ed. H. Foley, 43–57. New York: 1981.

Winkler, John J. *The Constraints of Desire*. New York: 1989.

# Portrait of Sappho
## by Paul Roche

### 1

TWELVE HUNDRED YEARS of ancient testimony
(roughly 600 B.C. to 600 A.D.) insisted that Sappho
was the greatest woman poet[1] the world had known
and, with her male contemporaries, Anacreon and
Alcaeus, one of the greatest practitioners—perhaps
*the* greatest practitioner—of love poetry. The enthusi-
asm of some ancient testimony goes so far as to rank
her as second only to Homer and to refer to her as
"the tenth Muse," but it is doubtful that this repre-
sents the concensus of appraisal in antiquity.

However that may be, and for reasons that are
uncertain, the fact is that very little of Sappho's poetry
was still extant by the end of the eleventh century A.D.
It has often been supposed that her works were ex-
punged from the libraries in several bursts of puritani-
cal zeal by Christian zealots, and there is some truth in
this, but she was still being read by prominent literati
(Christian no doubt) in the late fourth century, and
right up to the sixth and seventh centuries copies were
still being made of her poems. What is likely is that
however Sappho may have suffered from the censor-
ship of bigots, the chief cause of her extinction was the
same as that which consigned to oblivion vast quanti-
ties of classical literature, namely: chance, neglect,
changes in school syllabuses, library fires, political and
historical upheavals.

These things being so, only a glimmer of Sappho's
tenuous and passionate humanity came down to us,
shining through the arid pages of grammarians, metricists,
and professional critics. Yet the impetus of that first

universal affirmation—though the world had little more to go on than two poems and a handful of fragments— lasted somehow to our own day. It seemed impossible that even if a parchment or papyrus had escaped the ravages of zealots, it could have escaped the ravages of time. Only in the dry air of Egypt, somewhere under the waterless sands, was it conceivable that further treasures of Sappho lay buried and conserved.

Then miraculously in 1879, in the oasis of Fayum in the Nile valley, a breakthrough in classical discoveries occurred. Manuscripts of the eighth century A.D. came to light and some of these proved to be poems by Sappho. This was followed in 1897 through 1906 by an extensive series of excavations undertaken by the Egypt Exploration Society, when two English professors, B.P. Grenfell and A.S. Hunt, digging in the ancient refuse heaps of Aphroditopolis and Oxyrhynchus (110 miles south-southwest of Cairo),[2] unearthed unparalleled quantities of papyruses ranging from the first century B.C. to the tenth A.D. Many of these turned out to be fragments of Sappho. The papyrus rolls had been torn into strips and used as a kind of papier-mâché to make the cartonage of coffins, or used as a lining for mummies, or wadded into the carcasses of crocodiles and other stuffed, sacred animals.

The discovery, assembling and deciphering of these finds has become one of the most exciting developments in modern paleography.[3] A battery of international scholars has continued to work on the fragments and on others found since. Progress is slow but every few years there is released to the world a further trickle of texts. Although we still have only about one twentieth of what Sappho wrote, we are beginning at last to measure her status as a poet on more than mere hearsay.

## 2

What then is the aura, the magic, the unmistakable perfume that is Sappho? That which made Meleager, introducing his famous "garland" of poems and epigrams in the first century B.C., write: ". . . of Sappho only a few, but all roses;" and Strabo putting together his Geography at about the same time exclaim: "In all recorded history I know of no woman who came even close to Sappho as a poet."

As everyone who has tried, I found her impossible to translate. The limpidity yet intenseness, precision yet musicality, fluidity yet formality of her Greek, lures translators toward one or two grotesque extremes —either imitation William Carlos Williams or pseudo-Swinburnian: the one cut to the bone, the other decked out to the last flourish and flounce of art-for-art's-sake.

And yet Sappho is a modern: modern in the sense that Beowulf, The Faerie Queene, and even Tennyson are not. Her setting may not be ours, but the manner of her sensibility is. Her reflective, self-critical, self-dramatizing persona could be a Virginia Woolf's or a Sylvia Plath's. Her immediate response to the beauty of dawn or the way a little girl picks flowers, the glance over her shoulder to watch her own passionate commitments as if they did not concern her, her tongue-in-cheek commentary on her own naïveté, even the burst of intolerance with which she responds to the sounds of mourning around her sickbed; all this— warm, impatient, amused, detached—mark her as a modern.

What is more, her style is simple; at least she makes us think it simple. She uses almost no metaphors and sometimes no adjectives (No. 171 is a notable example.) And though on occasion she can ascend Mount Parnassus to intone in the grand epic utterance (No. 82), generally she eschews a poetic vocabulary and writes in her own Aeolian vernacular. Neither a romantic nor a symbolizer of abstruse themes, she deals with love, friendship, and affection in a way that creates the illusion of naturalness itself while often being amazingly subtle. Some of the fragments are epigrams crystalizing wisdom (Nos. 113, 126, 127, 159); many more celebrate human relations from passion, through intoxication, to despair—with tenderness, pity, sarcasm, anger, and sadness in between.

Prosodically as tightly controlled as a sonnet or a

villanelle, Sappho's verse manages nevertheless to be spontaneous with a conversational directness. It has all the projective immediacy that Ferlinghetti, Corso, Ginsberg, and the Beat poets mustered when they first hit the world, but with a verbal artistry as bold and as disciplined as Gerard Manley Hopkins's. In sonic vigor alone, in sheer audial design, "They charm and seduce," as Plutarch wrote. Yes, "Her songs bewitch the ear." Nobody before or since has ever got closer to making art appear artless while keeping it artifice.

In spite of all this, Sappho has not been without critics from the ranks of those very scholars who have sought to reassess her. The late Denys Page of Cambridge, for instance, (the most erudite perhaps of those who have written recently on Greek lyrical poetry), was almost dismissive in his appraisal of Sappho's poetry. Unimpressed with her subject matter, he says of the deceptively simple No. 53 ("For even in Sardis our dear Anactoria . . .") that it is "devoid of anything profound in thought or emotion or memorable language."[4] Others have found her homely or trite and her language verging on prose: as if the same strictures might not just as reasonably be leveled against Jane Austen, Emily Dickinson or Gertrude Stein. For it is precisely in the ordinariness of their material and the extraordinariness they distill from it that the originality of these writers lies.

Perhaps this lack of enthusiasm stems from forgetting that Sappho wrote songs, she wrote for the ear, with all the need for repetition and the quickly recognized phrase that song requires. Besides which, many of her images and similes, which for us have become near clichés, were being minted for the first time. Nor must one forget that she was not merely trying to say something but to *make* something: to make a design out of words as remarkable for its own sake as a painting or a piece of sculpture. (For my part, should I ever come to read Sappho aloud in the Greek and not succumb to the miracle of her aural effects, I hope I should still be sensate enough to brand myself as tone-deaf.)

---

But Sappho's poems were not just read aloud, they were sung or recited to the accompaniment of the lyre all over Greece and throughout the Mediterranean. Probably they were also mimed and danced. Music and the making of music, together with rhythm, movement, and gesture, went hand in hand with the making of poetry. Stringed instruments were advanced, various, and popular. The island of Lesbos was already a fount of poetry and song when Sappho was born there sometime between 630 and 612 B.C. Homer himself (alive to every Greek, though some hundred years dead) came from the neighboring coastlands. Arion and Terpander (who is credited with adding three strings to the four-stringed lyre) had shortly preceded her. Alcaeus, whose lyrics were almost as famous as hers, was her contemporary and admirer. But what made Sappho the most important poet after Homer and before Pindar—not forgetting Alcaeus—was that under her the art of lyric poetry reached a summit of perfection before any of the sister arts in Athens or the mainland. (One has only to look at the sculpture of the seventh and sixth century B.C. to see how "primitive" in contrast it is.) Sappho set her songs to her own accompaniment on the lyre and the πηκτίς (pēctis —a small harp, which she seems to have been the first to use, as also the *plectrum.*) She may not have invented the *Sapphic meter,* but her development of it was so individual that it became associated with her name forever.

### 3

So, what kind of island was it on which Sappho was born somewhere toward the last quarter of the seventh century B.C.? Beautiful certainly, more beautiful than it is now. The voracious shipbuilding programs of ambitious states had not yet shorn every island in the Aegean of its trees. The still more voracious goat (following the wake of the charcoal burner in search of saplings) had not yet clipped to the ground the greenery of hill and valley. Lesbos was a well-wooded, well-watered, well-populated island: already one of the jewels of early Hellenic civilization. Its capital, Mytilene, a mere stone's throw from the opulence of the Orient, was a center of trade and culture. It faced the fashionable town of Sardis, only a day's journey away on the mainland of Asia Minor.

The temper of the island was undoubtedly aristocratic, governed as it was by a handful of distinguished families. Sappho's husband was a rich businessman from the island of Andros, and her brother Charaxus (she had three brothers[5]) made himself prosperous shipping wine from Lesbos to the Greek colony of Naucratis in Egypt. For all we know, the series of stinging letters in which she berated him (in perfect sapphics) for going off with the famous courtesan Rhodopis (Rosycheeks) was part of her deep psychological repugnance for the vulgarity of "modern" living. And although she by no means despised money (Nos. 126, 127), she could cripple with words of immemorial cruelty the memory of one who had money but no culture.

> Dead, you'll lie there, woman, unregarded:
>     no one to recall you ever after—
> You who had no share
>     of the roses from Pieria.
> Feeble in the cellars of Lord Death,
>     obscure even there,
> You'll flit among uncelebrated dead.

Although we know very little of Sappho's life for certain, we can reconstruct with some degree of probability the main lines of it, and with even greater probability its manner and style. Her husband may have died early in their married life, for he is not mentioned in the extant poetry. Of children, she had one, a daughter called Cleïs, (Brilliant).

> I have a pretty little girl
> Lovely as a golden flower,
> Cleïs, whom I so adore

I would not take all Lydia
(Nor Lesbos even lovelier)
In exchange for her.

It is Cleïs whom she addresses in a papyrus of the
third century B.C., (by far the oldest extant papyrus of
Sappho) written probably when the tyrant Myrsilus
had wrested power from the aristocratic oligarchy and
forced Sappho to take up residence in the small town
of Pyrrha in the center of Lesbos. The shops of Mytilene
were now inaccessible to mother and daughter. Sappho
thinks wistfully of the remnants of their finery, sym-
bols, and memorials of happier days.

> My mother would say that when she was young
> Nothing could touch a crimson band
>
> Looped through the hair—and no denying—
> But a girl with hair like a fall of flame
>
> Couldn't do better than a crown of flowers . . .
> Anyway, Cleïs, I don't have a thing
>
> Like a gorgeous Sardian headband now
> And not the slightest idea of where
>
> (With the Cleanax clan controlling town)
> A gorgeous headband can be found . . .
>
> Of course our Mytilenian remnants are
> All rotted away.

Apparently because of her family's political affini-
ties, Sappho was banished at least once, possibly twice.
On one occasion she went to Sicily and took up resi-
dence in Syracuse,[6] which was rapidly becoming one
of the wealthiest cities in the Mediterranean—the New
York of the ancient world. Its citizens felt so honored
by her visit that later they put up a statue to her.[7] Still
probably in her early twenties at the most, Sappho
must have proceeded through Greece as a celebrity, a
"star," meeting some of the most important people of
her time: "a miracle of a young woman" as Strabo put
it some centuries later. Even the great Solon, law-

giver, ruler, poet (the Thomas Jefferson of his age) sang her praises and one evening after the wine when his nephew sang a song of Sappho's, he turned to the boy and said: "Teach me that song." "Whatever for?" one of the company asked. "Because I want to learn it and die."

In all this it is worth noting that the social standing of women in seventh- and sixth-century Lesbos appears to have been different from what it was or became on the mainland of Hellas. There are indications that the ladies of Lesbos were far from being mere appendages of their husbands and comported themselves with an autonomy not to be seen again until the later days of the Roman Empire. Though commerce, war, and athletic prowess were the obvious concerns of men, this had not yet driven an irretrievable wedge between the sexes. Women moved and spoke freely among men, appeared publicly at festivals, were asked their opinion, and gave it. The tension between male and female implicit in Sappho's poetry (as Josephine Balmer* illustrates so well) had not yet led to the wholesale devaluation of women. Sappho fearlessly parades the virtues and excellence of her sex. In No. 42, for instance, Helen of Troy is not the naughty woman who caused the fall of Ilium, but something of a heroine who gave a supreme lesson in single-minded love. And in the marriage songs it is the bride who is celebrated rather than the bridegroom: *she* is the prize that the young man has prayed for and been lucky enough to win.

## 4

But what of Sappho's manner of life after she had reestablished herself at Mytilene: in that island so richly wooded with pine and chestnut, groves of the evergreen ilex and the ubiquitous olive? Contemporary scholars exhibit a particular dislike of the theory

*Sappho, Poems & Fragments, by Josephine Balmer. (Meadowland Books 1984).

that held sway among yesterday's scholars: that of Sappho the director of a semireligious academy for girls, whose interest centered on the worship of Aphrodite and the Muses.

It is more probable that Sappho and the other ladies of Lesbos tended to form their own groups to talk about and do the things nearest their hearts, just as the men did—whose interests were more likely to be trade, sport, politics, and war.

Be that as it may, Lesbos was famous as the home both of women of refinement and of song. Sappho was the most notable illustration of both. Sappho loved young companions. It was the tradition for women and girls to sing and dance at festivals. The latter had to be trained, "finished" in the ways of art and excellence. With such a dynamic personality behind them, the girls became bound to her and to one another in an intimacy loyal, dramatic, and tense. And in a world that believed in the proximity of divine forces—friendly and unfriendly—they cultivated the dieties that interested them most: Aphrodite and the Muses.

And so there grew up around Sappho an entourage of young girls who came and went, sent (presumably) by their parents. They came from Lesbos and from farther afield, from all over Asia Minor and the Aegean islands. We know the names of many of them: Anactoria, the subject of two of Sappho's loveliest odes; Gongyla, from Colophon near Ephesus; Timas of Phocaea, who died young and far from home; Euneika from the island of Salamis near Athens; Hero of Gyara, near the island of Andros; and from Lesbos itself: Atthis, Praxinoa, Telessippa, Cydro, Mnasidika (or Dika), Archeanassa, and Pleistodike. There were also, coming from where we do not know: Gyrinno, Erinna, Megara, Anagora, and Micca.

These girls stayed until it was time for them to marry. Then Sappho would find herself not only pouring out poignant verses of regret at their going, but also furnishing the young couple with their wedding songs.

Given Sappho's vivid expression of her feelings toward

her own sex, an expression that paints an indelible picture of sheer intoxication at the approach of physical beauty, we must at least touch on the inevitable question of whether Sappho was a lesbian in the modern sense of the word: a word, incidentally, that came into play in English from a medical dictionary only as late as 1890.

It is perhaps unfortunate that so much ink has been spattered over this question, since it arouses emotional responses that become an obstacle to the poems themselves. Each generation tends to read Sappho in its own way, thereby telling us more about itself than about her work. We have no idea, for instance, what poems unleashed the fury of certain elements in the Christian Church, but we do know that if it was triggered by any of her extant work, or simply on mere hearsay, that fury was an expression of bigotry. Similarly the minds and mores of nineteenth-century scholars are laid bare in their passionate attempt to see no homosexual element in her poetry and therefore in her life. Just as today our own conclusions about Sappho tend to reflect a more liberated age. In any case, it is always dangerous to draw autobiographical conclusions from a poet's work, because writers in general can just as easily create an experience from their imagination as build upon fact.

There is no doubt, however, that Sappho was swayed by the beauty and presence of her own sex, even though there are indications that she was by no means immune to the attractions of men. Yet in one of her most famous lyrics she admits to being dizzy with frustration at the sight of the bridegroom sitting opposite one of her favorites.

> He is a god in my eyes, that man,
> Given to sit in front of you
> And close to himself sweetly to hear
>     The sound of you speaking.
>
> Your magical laughter—this I swear—
> Batters my heart—my breast astir.
> My voice when I see you suddenly near
>     Refuses to come.

My tongue breaks up and a delicate fire
Runs through my flesh; I see not a thing
With my eyes, and all that I hear
    In my ears is a hum.

The sweat runs down, a shuddering takes
Me in every part, and pale as the drying
Grasses, then, I think I am near
    The moment of dying.

It is curious that by the fourth and third centuries
B.C. the playwrights of the Middle and New Comedy
have turned Sappho from a literary into a sexual ce-
lebrity, and that by the first century A.D. Horace and
Ovid[8] talk suggestively of her and lesbianism as if they
were inevitably linked in men's minds: curious because
they seem to have forgotten that Sappho had com-
posed the greatest body of heterosexual songs in antiq-
uity: processional chants, bridal farewells, ribald catches
for the feast, and the actual celebration of union be-
tween man and maid.

However one resolves these paradoxes, one must
remember that homosexuality was no disgrace among
the ancient Greeks. We must be just as much on our
guard against those who would debilitate the passion
for her own sex that could sweep over Sappho, as
those who would inject into such feelings a post-
Christian sense of sin and shame. There must have
been an innocence in Sappho's relations with her own
sex that knew no shame, because it knew no guilt. If
she uttered the words below, heavily reconstructed by
J.M. Edmonds as they are, I believe that she spoke
the truth.

And I said to them: "Sweet women,
    how you will remember always
        till you are old
The things we did together
    in shining youth.
For many the things we did then
    innocent beautiful.
And now that you go from here
    my heart is breaking.

---

Although, as I have said, we know very little of
Sappho's actual life, it is difficult not to feel after
perusing her poems and fragments that we know a
great deal about *Sappho*. In my translation I have
arranged them in a sequence that quite surprised me
by its cumulative power if one reads the whole se-
quence aloud: (indispensable in a poetry as sonant as
Sappho's). Sappho herself seems to step into the light
and one begins to think one knows even what she
looked like. Alas, of this we can never be sure. The
three or four busts of her that exist are all several
centuries too late, as are the effigies of her on
Mytilenian and Roman coins. The fact that she is
described in antiquity both as beautiful and ill-favored[9]
suggests that she may have been one of those women
who, like great actresses, project an illusion of beauty
and by the spirit, grace and sparkling integrity of their
persons are more captivating than the merely beauti-
ful; though there is often something formidable about
this kind of allure. Alcaeus, that attractive but roister-
ous character who was some twelve years younger
than Sappho, once said to her:

Violet-decked, virtuous, honey-sweet smiling Sappho,
I've something to tell you, but, ah, shame stops me!

And Sappho answered (in his own meter, not hers,
thus implying a smile):

If you were after the good and the fair, sir,
and your tongue were not concocting a guilty message,
you wouldn't have shame in your eyes, sir,
but say your say like an honest man.

**6**

When we come to consider the latter part and the
mysterious end of Sappho's life, we find it full of
nostalgia and a sense of valediction. How she died and
when, or even where, is shrouded in doubt. Arthur

Weigall is one of the few writers who believes and tries to substantiate the story of her futile love-chase of the young sailor, Phaon. Another is Peter Green, who lived on the island of Lesbos and wrote a plausible if somewhat romantic reconstruction of Sappho's life called *The Laughter of Aphrodite*.

Weigall conjectures the date as not before 558 B.C. and calculates that Sappho was in her "early fifties—woman's most tragic age, when beauty wanes but longing is not gone . . . One must suppose her to have been no older than that at the time of her death, and no younger, either, as is shown by her sad description of her increasing wrinkles, and her admission that she is beyond the age of childbearing." (Nos. 158 & 152). It was the case of the aging, brilliant woman grasping at the last possibility of admiration and love.

According to this story, the young Phaon—an adept at breaking hearts among the Aeolian ladies—was at first flattered that the most famous woman in the world had succumbed to his good looks but eventually grew tired of her and left abruptly for Sicily. Sappho set out to follow him but when she reached the island of Leucas (south of Corfu and on the direct sailing route via Corinth for Sicily), the sadness and hopelessness of her plight overwhelmed her and she threw herself over the Leucadian promontary: a spot already famous for ritual suicides. Her body was reverently retrieved from the rocks and brought back to Lesbos.

It makes a romantic story, believed apparently by Menander in the fourth century B.C., Plautus in the third century B.C., and Ovid in the first A.D. But perhaps they all got it from the same source. In any event, it seems now fairly well accepted that Phaon was a δαιμών (daimōn: a semidivine or mythological personage) associated with Aphrodite. He was "a ferryman plying for hire between Lesbos and the mainland, and one day he ferried over for nothing the goddess Venus (Aphrodite) in the guise of an old woman. For this she gave him an alabaster jar of unguent the daily use of which made women fall in love with him."[10] Sappho's incorporation into the story may be based on a later misunderstanding. According to other ancient commentators a "Sappho" did indeed fall in love with, pursue, and throw herself over a cliff for, the disdainful Phaon, but this was a celebrated courtesan of the same name, not Sappho the poet.

However Sappho may have died, her tomb in Lesbos is mentioned more than once in antiquity. Maximus of Tyre (a philosopher and rhetorician, c. A.D. 125–185) speaks of her deathbed and quotes her as rebuking her daughter Cleïs for weeping, (No. 170). But we have no way of knowing whether this was her real or putative deathbed. The fact that she was able to write a poem about it suggests that on this occasion she recovered.

> The sounds of mourning do not suit
> a house that serves the Muse.
> They are not wanted here.

The value of our Greek and Roman past is that it shows us what we are by what we once were. It shows us what is constant in our growth. We cannot break that continuity. We cannot lose our memory and live. Sappho and Homer are harbingers of the Greek spirit, the civilized spirit, whereby we choose to cultivate the three elemental quotients of the fulfilled and examined life: a quest for the beautiful, a sense of leisure, and the pursuit of freedom.

Sappho in the perfection of her art, recorded, recreated, condensed, and lifted to a lyrical plane all that it means to suffer the glory and the sting of being a woman—and in love. But she does more. Within that vision she shows us by her untrammeled response and wholeness of person, all that it means to be human.

> Yes
> they gave me true success
> the golden
> Muses
> And once dead
> I shall not be forgotten.

---

Many have been cheated by oblivion
but by good judges
none.

And afterwards, I say,
I shall be remembered:
oh certainly, by some.

The understanding gods evoke tears.
But for me, listen well:
My delight is the exquisite.
Yes, for me
Glitter and sunlight and love
are one society.

. . . passion, yes
. . . utterly, I can
. . . shall be to me
. . . a face
. . . shining back at me
. . . beautiful . . . indelibly

The moon has gone
The Pleiades gone
In dead of night
Time passes on
I lie alone.

# Translator's Preface

IT HAS BEEN well and often said that poetry is what gets lost in translation: the timbre and valency and color of words, with all the reverberations of their untrackable associations. One language cannot take a photograph of another, that is, reproduce it. The most it can do is represent it, which in poetry means recreating it.

Confronted with the perennial challenge of transferring the perfection of one language into the perfection of another, I have done my best to get near not only to what Sappho said but the way she said it. I have tried to catch the penumbra of her spontaneity, her sharpness and jewelry of sound. Of course, this is only an illusion.

When a poetry is stripped of its original music, a completely new set of sounds and rhythms has to be found. It is not that English is inferior to Greek for the expression of feelings and concepts, but that it is different. Sappho can be plain and ornate at the same time, in the same line, in the very same phrase. In Greek this is possible: possible to combine plain statement with sensuous and suggestive syllabic patterns. In English it is not. That is why we try to make up for it by a superfluity of metaphors. English can be plain in sound and plain in content. What English cannot easily be is plain in content and ornate in sound. I know of no way of saying: "Please come in, take a chair, and sit down," and making it sound like the cooing of turtledoves in spring. In Greek, with its syllabic richness and purity of vowels, its languorous diphthongs, its athletic grammatical inflections (which free the word order for euphony,) its shifting affixes of preposition that can change the whole nuance of a word in the twinkling of an eye, its mobility and pace (because it is not stodgy with consonants) . . . *that* precisely is what one can do; or at least what Sappho could. She has left all us translators limping behind.

In the Appendix I go into more detail on some of the problems of following her. Let me say here only that I have tried to give some idea of the variety within her verbal fabric, her flux of textures. I have tried to keep from being the same in all places and to reflect a little of her elusiveness, shift of tempos, subtleties of echo within technique and mood. Sappho was not an Imagist, though she uses images. She was not a Hopkins or a Swinburne, though she is rich in assonance and alliteration. Finally, she was not (as I earlier implied in "Portrait of Sappho") a William Carlos Williams or a Beat poet, though nobody could be more direct.

Meanwhile, as if the problems of translating were not serious enough, textual scholarship has seen to it that in this field, where the fragments are scarcer than diamonds, there should be a plethora of texts, readings, emendations, counter emendations, glosses, reconstructions and repudiations of reconstructions: a plethora enough to plague and delay the confused translator. I know what Mary Barnard must have felt when in a footnote to her own remarkable version* she says: "The texts vary to such an extent and have been emended by so many hands that the translator has a choice of words and meanings for almost every line."[11] The harassed translator puts his faith in one or two authorities and in sheer despair docilely follows. My own authorities have been chiefly Edmonds, Page, and Campbell (and sometimes Haines and Hill), though I have not always followed them nor always been

*Sappho*, by Mary Barnard, University of California Press, 1958.

docile. On occasion I have even added my own mite to the world's stock of emendations. A poet's nose, with perhaps no more than a modicum of scholarship, can sometimes lead one to a find, or what one hopes is a find. (See note to No. 53.)

We have, of course, none of the original papyruses on which Sappho herself wrote; if indeed she did write her poems down, which is not improbable. Our earliest papyrus is of the third century B.C., i.e. about three hundred years after her death, though there is a shard, a piece of pottery, inscribed in a hand of the fourth century. Her popularity wherever Greek was spoken ensured that her work was transcribed by hundreds of different hands, often probably fresh from the lips of professional singers as they sang or recited the words to the strings of the lyre. Since the poems were short, they were probably often written down from memory—a method of publication which in itself was a fertile seedbed for variant readings.

Sappho is reputed to have composed nine books of poems (as arranged by the Alexandrian scholars centuries later according to meter) consisting of wedding lays, epigrams, elegeia, and lyric monodies called μξλη (melë). I have collected most of what there is, and I have not disdained to use the "restored" texts. Without them it is impossible to give any coherent impression of what Sappho felt and sang about, since so many of the papyrus rolls have been torn across and we have only one or other half of the whole stanzas. However, where the degree of restoration has reached the point of pure conjecture, I say so in the notes. These reconstructions—the work of Grenfell, Hunt, Wilamowitz-Moellendorff, Edmonds, Diehl, Lobel, and others—follow paleographical methods, which are a science in themselves. It is noteworthy that when a recent find has by good fortune duplicated a papyrus we already possess, the restoration has sometimes proved to be correct. In further apologia I think it fair to say that even in the most conjectural of the restored passages, where it is far from certain how Sappho expressed herself, there is seldom the same degree of doubt as to the gist of what she said. One does not question that in places where the records are blank, it is frivolous to fill in the gaps with fancy; but neither should one question that without recourse to "historical imagination" it is impossible to make any human sense of the records at all. One must remember that the truth that the textual scholar pursues resides in the unquestionable certainty of the text; but the truth which the historian and translator pursue resides in finding out what probably happened. These two truths are not always the same, indeed can contradict each other—as I show in my commentary of No. 119. For these reasons, I have continued to base my translation on the Edmonds's text even though, from the purely scholarly point of view, as Dr. David Campbell in the Preface to his own edition, (with perhaps charitable understatement), says: the "Edmonds's version of the papyrus texts was spoiled by his excessive eagerness to fill the gaps."

I have arranged my *Sappho* in six different "books," roughly following the line of her moods and ending with the touching nostalgia of her middle and old age. The effect, as I have said, is cumulative: designed to give as vivid a play as possible to her varied personality. If the method appears arbitrary (poems being brought together that possibly were in quite different books in her own arrangement,) I can only say that we have no idea what Sappho's own arrangement was and that a division of books according to meter carries no guarantee of being less arbitrary. My method has this to it, that where so much is fragmentary it helps to compensate for all we are losing, and it produces a certain unity of movement.

Lastly, let me acknowledge that I have followed the lead of Ms. Barnard in providing headings for most of the poems and fragments. These are probabilities suggested by the context in which the poem was quoted in antiquity, or otherwise conjectured from Sappho's own background. The headings are supplementary and supply the sense of missing lines, besides giving a setting and a sequence to what otherwise would be unfocused.

# NOTES TO "PORTRAIT OF SAPPHO" AND TRANSLATOR'S PREFACE

1. Little is known of the other women poets of the centuries B.C. The names usually cited are: Corinna, Damophyla, Praxilla, Erinna, Anyte, Myrtis, and Nossis. Corinna is credited with having defeated Pindar in several contests. Characteristically her victories were put down to her beauty rather than to her art. Ironically in one of the two surviving fragments of her verse, she rebukes Myrtis for daring to compete with Pindar when "she was only a woman." Certainly none of these women ever achieved Sappho's reputation.

2. Of Oxyrhynchus itself very little is known. The town was a Greco-Egyptian provincial capital and what remains of it is hardly more than a series of mounds.

3. The papyruses have found their way into various museums around the world: notably the Cairo Museum, the British Museum, and the Louvre; also in the United States. Meanwhile, the work of the Egypt Exploration Society is supplemented in other countries by the Berlin Academy, the Società Italiana, and the Graeca Halensis.

4. For a compelling defense of this poem, see *Sappho, Poems and Fragments*, by Josephine Balmer.

5. Of Sappho's three brothers, Larichus, the youngest, is said to have had his praises sung by Sappho for being cupbearer in the town hall of Mytilene, (which means he was young and good-looking). We know nothing of Eurygyus, but Charaxus was the one berated by his sister for squandering himself over the celebrated courtesan Rhodopis (also known as Doricha).

6. It must be remembered that Sicily and the whole of southern Italy was Greek. Indeed, the latter was known as Magna Graeca (Greater Greece). Even in living memory a species of Greek was still to be heard in some of the villages of lower Calabria. As to Syracuse, it is interesting to note that Theocritus, the father of pastoral poetry, lived there during the third century B.C., and also about the same time Archimedes, the greatest mathematician and inventor of antiquity.

7. Cicero, in 56 B.C., inveighing against the corrupt Verres, who had been Roman governor of Sicily, charged him among various crimes of extortion with having stolen the statue of Sappho from the town hall in Syracuse: a statue, he said, "not only beautifully done but with a famous sapphic epigram on the base." (So powerful was Cicero's indictment that Verres did not wait for the outcome of the case but fled to the country, where he lived in affluence till he was assassinated.)

8. Ovid wrote: *"Lesbia quid docuit Sappho nisi amare puellas?"* ("What did Sappho of Lesbos teach except how to love girls?") Ovid however was ambivalent, he also believed the story of Sappho's love-chase of the handsome Phaon, the young man who ferried people between Lesbos and the mainland. (Alexander Pope made a famous translation of Ovid's poem on the subject in 1707:

I burn, I burn, as when through ripened corn
By driving winds the spreading flames are borne.
Phaon to Aetna's scorching fields retires,
While I consume with more than Aetna's fires . . .

As to Horace, he wrote: "The masculine Sappho adapts her Muse to the measures of Archilochus." (A poet a little earlier than Sappho who was famous for the vigor and vehemence of his odes and satires.)

9. Maximus of Tyre, philosopher and historian of the first century, wrote: " 'The beautiful Sappho,' is

what Socrates liked to call her because of the beauty of her songs, although she was really small and dark." Damochares, professional critic of the first century, commenting on a protrait of Sappho, wrote: "Oh painter, Nature herself gave you the Pierian Muse of Mytilene to portray! What clarity is in her eyes, and how this blazons forth her imagination and intelligence! Her skin, which you have painted so naturally, is smooth and shows forth her simplicity. Her features mingle joyous-ness with wit, manifesting the Muse and Cypris (Aphrodite) joined in one." (As quoted in the *Palatine Anthology,* a tenth century collection of quotations compiled from ancient sources.)
10. Servius, critic and historian of the first century, writing on the *Aeneid.*
11. *Sappho,* by Mary Barnard, 1958.

# The Love Songs

# BOOK I

## *Overtures of Loving*

### I

#### WINGED WORDS

Winged words
Words made of air
I begin
But words good to hear

### 2

#### THIS IS A PROMISE

I'll sing these songs
beautifully
today
to please you
my faithful coterie

## 3

### WHEN I OPENED MY EYES

Hardly had Eos
goddess of dawn
in golden slippers
touched me

## 4

My lady Dawn

## 5

### LAST NIGHT I SAID TO HIM

Oneirus, god of dreams,
son of the jet black night,
last lingerer as the morning light
lifts slumber from our eyes—you soothing god
who warns me of the tension and the strife
of keeping burning wish and act apart:
I do not think that I shall spurn
the truth of what you've shown.
For with the Blessed Ones' support
I shall by no means not
grasp the thing for which I groan.
When I was a little child
I never was so imbecile
as turn my back upon a bauble
my loving mother held towards me.
So let the Blessed Ones, I pray, and presently,
provide me with the chance
of what I crave:
seeing that I've honored them in poetry
and in my dance.

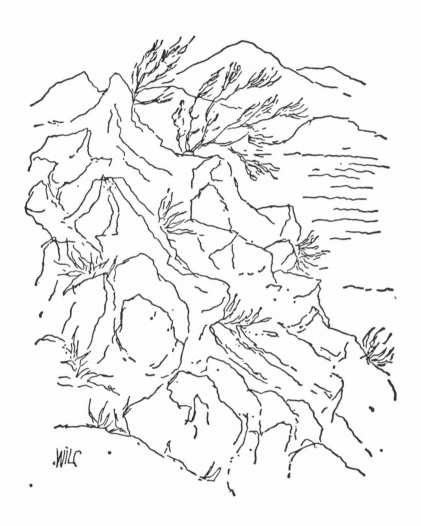

## 6

### WE SIGH

O for Adonis!

## 7

### BUT NOT EVERYBODY WANTS LOVE

Young Artemis swore a great oath:
"A virgin forever I *shall* be,
Pure on the peaks of the mountains.
Father, for my sake, agree."
And the Father of the Blessed Immortals
Nodded assent. On Olympus
She is known to the gods as Deer-shooter,
Goddess of wilderness: title
Great in renown. And the god
Who never comes near her is Love.

## 8

### I AM LISTENING FOR

That telltale of the spring:
the melody-making nightingale

## 9

AND WAITING FOR EROS

The dearest scion
of Earth and Heaven

## 10

IN SPRING

Earth in many crowns
vests in her crowded brocade

## 11

BUT I WASTE MY TIME

It's useless
trying to bend
a stubborn heart

## 12

The ones I have helped
hurt me most

## 13

ONCE AGAIN APHRODITE

I have run to you fluttering
like a little girl to her mother

## 14

AND TO YOU SWEET PEITHO

Man-beguiler: daughter of Aphrodite

## 15

I SAID

Sappho
Why do you turn your back
on the exquisite blessings of Aphrodite?

## 16

I shall go—unleashed, unpegged

## 17

## SO I CALLED TO APHRODITE

Undying Aphrodite on your caparisoned throne,
Daughter of Zeus and weaver of ruses—
    Now I address you:

Queen, do not hurt my heart, do not harry it
But come as before when you heard and you hearkened
    A long way away,

And leaving behind the house of your father,
Harnessed a golden chariot winged
    By your beautiful swans,

Beating and whirring across the sky,
Bringing you down to the unbright earth—
    So suddenly there:

Mistress, the smile on your undying features
Asking me what was it troubled me this time?
    What made me call you

This time? What was my desperate heart wanting done?
And your: "Whom shall I this time bend to your love?
    Who is it Sappho

That's doing you wrong? For if she's escaping
Soon she'll be chasing; if she's refusing
    Your gifts, she shall give them.

And if she's not loving, soon shall she love you,
Like it or no." . . . Oh, come again now:
Let me go loose from this merciless craving.
Do what I long to have done: be my own
    Helper in Battle.

## 18

COME WHEREVER YOU ARE

Whether at Cyprus and Paphos
Or at Panormus


## 19

I famish
and I pine


## 20

Pain drips


## 21

You scorch me


## 22

SHE CAME RADIANT

In a spangled gown
of Lydian design
quite beautiful
reaching down
to her toes

---

## 23

THE MOMENT I SAW HER

Love
like a sudden breeze
tumbling on the oak-tree leaves
left my heart
trembling

## 24

And they laughed—the immortal gods

## 25

How did you wound so easily?

## 26

Sing us the praises
of the girl with the violet-sweet breasts

## 27

### I MORE THAN ENVY HIM

He is a god in my eyes, that man,
Given to sit in front of you
And close to himself sweetly to hear
    The sound of you speaking.

Your magical laughter—this I swear—
Batters my heart—my breast astir—
My voice when I see you suddenly near
    Refuses to come.

My tongue breaks up and a delicate fire
Runs through my flesh; I see not a thing
With my eyes, and all that I hear
    In my ears is a hum.

The sweat runs down, a shuddering takes
Me in every part and pale as the drying
Grasses, then, I think I am near
    The moment of dying

**28**

### I'M BAFFLED

I do not know
what to do
my mind's
in two

**29**

IT'S TOO HIGH

I do not aspire
with my two arms
to touch the sky

**30**

COME

And I shall set you to rest
on the softest of cushions:
Yes, you shall lie
on fresh new pillows

**31**

I WANT

Darling, to hug you

**32**

IN HOMAGE

Stars round the fair moon
veil their own shining
when she's full on the earth
with the light of her silver

---

## 33

**MAY I SAY**

I think no girl
that sees the sun
will ever equal you in skill

## 34

**ARE YOU**

Forgetting me?

## 35

**TELL ME FRANKLY**

Is there any man
anywhere among mankind
you love more than me?

## 36

What will your eyes say?

# BOOK II
## *Petitions and Observations*

### 37

**AS WE LOVE YOU**

So
You
O Graces O
Irreproachable
Ones
With arms like roses!
Zeus's
Virgin daughters
Do
Approach us

### 38

**I CANNOT WRITE**

Heart, be still!
No jet of spellbound song,
no Adonis-hymn
streams out from you
beautifully, to please
the goddesses:
Desire the disconcerter,

Aphrodite the dictator
of hearts, has made you dumb;
and Peitho the enticer
from her flagon of gold
has flooded your thinking soul
with nectar


## 39

For us it is not easy
To rival goddesses
In sheer beauty,
But *you* . . .


## 40

### I AM TOO SUSCEPTIBLE

Yesterday, Children, I passed you
Huddled beneath the great bay tree.
The sight was a potion—I drained it;
A spasm of happiness seized me.
The women I walked with imagined
Me moody and silent and heedless.
At times I hardly could hear them:
All that I heard was my ears drum;
My spirit, poor darling, had flown.
These things it seems are of fate then.
I made up my mind, gentle creatures,
To see you, but then you had gone—
(Too quick by half in your tracks);
Though I glimpsed at a vision that thrilled me:
The clothes on your backs.

## WE NEED YOUR HELP

Hurry to us here, you Muses:
Good-bye to your golden mansions

## TO HERA

Form in a dream, my lady Hera,
Sweetest shape, O come before me:
Whom the Atreidae—kings of glory—
 Prayed and conjured

When their sack of Troy was over.
On first launching out for home
From Scamander's swirling river,
 They were thwarted

Till they begged you and the mighty
Zeus; Thyone's darling child too.
So I ask you, lady, also:
 Bring back olden

Ways I shared both pure and lovely
With my Mytilenian maidens:
The song, the dancing, once I taught them
 Round your feast days.

Even as the twins of Atreus
With your help and your divine ones
Sailed awy from Troy—so help me
 Home again, Hera

## 43

### DON'T LET IT HAPPEN TO ME

At the height of the storm the terrified sailors throw
Their cargoes out and ground their ship on the beach.

My God! I hope that *I* never have to go
Voyaging anywhere over the sea in the winter,

Or ever be forced to throw my goods and chattels
Into the brink: a shame! or *I'd* think so

If ever it happens to me that all my possessions
Fall to the swell of the sea and the Nereïds'
    processionals . . .

**44**

### IN MY DREAM, APHRODITE

A crimson handkerchief hung down
    your cheeks, the one
Timas sent to you from Phocaea:
    full of her adoration

**45**

### THE PLACE IS CALLING YOU, APHRODITE

Come to us here from Crete—to this holy
Temple: place of your own most pleasing
Apple groves and altars smoking
    Sweet with incense.

---

Here where the waters trickle coolly
Through apple boughs, and ground is shady
With roses, down from the leaves that shiver
    Sleep drops slowly.

Here is a meadow, horses feeding;
Spring profuse with flowers, and breezes
    Gently seeping.

Here then Cyprian goddess bring your
Lovable person; into golden
Goblets stir your nectar, mingling
    With our feasting

## 46

I talked in a dream
with Aphrodite

## 47

AND I SAID TO HER

Aphrodite, My Lady,
    crowned in gold,
        please
may that piece of luck be mine

## 48

### AS A TOKEN

I shall offer you
the rich burnt fat
of a white goat,
Yes, I shall leave it behind for you.

## 49

### AT LAST

You have come
and you did well to come
I pined for you.
And now you have put a torch to my heart
a flare of love—
O bless you and bless you and bless you:
you are back . . .
we were parted

## 50

### OPEN YOUR ARMS

Pretty One, I'm yours again:
far too long apart

## 51

### I AM AWED BY YOUR BEAUTY

For when I look upon you face-to-face
It seems Hermione even never was
One such as you:
                more like pale-haired Helen
I must say you are than any maid that dies.
And your tender beauty—O I shall confess—
I'd give all my thoughts in holocaust to it
And every sense for you in homage

## 52

### I COULD NOT WAIT

Yesterday you
Came to my house
And sang to me.
Now I
Come to you.
Talk to me. Do.
Lavish on me
Your own beauty.
For we walk to a wedding,
As well you know.
Please send away
Your maids. O may
Heaven then present me
With all that heaven ever meant for me.

### CONSOLE YOURSELF, ATTHIS

For even in Sardis our dear Anactoria
  Is sending her thoughts here:

Thoughts of the life we all led together when
You were to her a goddess descended
  And yours were the songs she adored.

Now far above the ladies of Lydia,
Like a moon at sunset rising dewy-
  Fingered among the stars and

Shedding her light on the salty sea
And over the flowery fields where the lovely
  Dewdrops lie and the roses

Rear and the lacy chervil blooms
With the melilot—so she wanders remembering
  Again and again her gentle

Atthis, till her tenuous heart is
Hung in her breast with a weight of longing;
  Till she cries to us: "Come!" and we

Hear it, and light-petaled night with its ears
Catches it, whispers it over the sea
  And all that's between

### SO I SHALL NEVER SEE HER!

Really, I'd rather be dead . . .
With a great many tears she left me saying:

"What a terrible blow—what sadness!
Sappho, I swear I leave you
Absolutely against my will."
And I said in reply:
"Go, be happy, good-bye.
Remember me—for you know how I loved you.

"Or if you do not I'll tell you
So many things you forget
Which made our life together a gladness:

"All the chaplets of sweet
Violets and rosebuds braided
And placed by you on your hair at my side.

"All the garlands woven
Around your delicate neck,
Fashioned from a hundred flowers.

"All the fragrance of myrrh
Fit for a queen and rare
Worn on your fresh young skin beside me,

"While on the softest beds
From the quiet hands of maids
No Ionian was so feted.

"There wasn't a single hill,
Holy purlieu, rill
From which we kept ourselves asunder.

"And never a wood in spring
Fretted with the crowded song
Of nightingales, where you and I
        Did not wander"

### TO A SOLDIER'S WIFE IN SARDIS: ANACTORIA

A cavalry corps, a column of men,
A flotilla in line, is the finest thing
In this rich world to see—for some . . . but for me
    It's the person you love.
There's nothing more easy than this to prove:
Helen whose beauty far outshone
The rest of man's chose to desert
    The best of men:

Willingly sailed away to Troy;
Thought nothing of child and nothing of fond
Parents, but was herself led astray
    By a love faraway;

(For woman is always easy to bend
The moment she's bent on her heart's desire.)
Now Anactoria's in my mind,
    Far from us here.

The way she walks, her lovable style,
The vivid movement of her face—
I'd rather see than Lydian horse
    And glitter of mail.

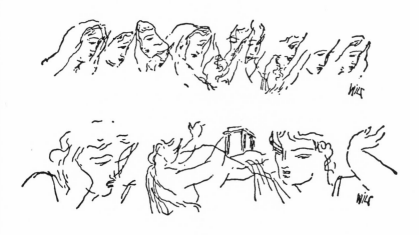

We cannot, alas, I know, have the best,
Yet to wish for a part of the past
Once shared is better for man at least
    Than that we forget

# BOOK III

## *Converse*

### 56

**IMAGES I REMEMBER**

**Once I saw a very gentle**
**very little**
**girl picking flowers**

### 57

**GOLDEN GENISTA**

**Grew along the shore**

### 58

**And the ripe marriageable girls wore garlands**

## 59

Girls with voices like honey

## 60

And the garlands were wild parsley

## 61

### THEN AT NOON

The cricket
from under his wings
struck forth his rapier-sweet songs
as the god of the sun poured down
on the earth his stream of flame

## 62

### IT GIVES ME JOY TO THINK

I have a pretty little girl
lovely as a golden flower;
Cleïs, whom I so adore
I would not take all Lydia
Nor Lesbos (even lovelier)
in exchange for *her*

---

## 63

### I BELIEVE I AM

More child-lover even than Gello
with her vampire thirst for children


## 64

Mnasidica has a prettier figure
then gentle Gyrinno


## 65

### TO MNASIDICA

You, Dicka, should weave wreaths with your delicate
    fingers
  Bind sprays of dill into your beautiful hair
  Surely even the glance of the blessed Graces
  Is more drawn to whatever is dressed with flowers
    Than to the ungarlanded?

### BUT FRANKLY DEAR

That was not right of you, Mika,
and I shall not let it pass:
your making overtures
to the house of Penthilos. . . .
Oh, what was that sweet noise—
That unseen honey-sound? . . .
A song-burst of nightingales:
Like drops of dew.


## 67

### YOU MAY SMILE BUT

Leda, they say,
once found an egg
hidden under a hyacinth


## 68

### WE ARE GOING TO DANCE

So come now
you delectable Graces
you Muses with the glorious tresses

## 69

### YES

I taught her well—
that Hero:
quick-sprinting girl
from Gyara

## 70

### WHAT IS

Far sweeter-tuned
than a lyre
Golder than gold
Softer than velvet
Much whiter
than an egg?

## 71

### APHRODITE'S WORDS WERE

". . . Eros my slave
and of course you too
Sappho"

## 72

So I am not the only woman
who haunts the Latmian Cave

## 73

I tell you, they have been generous with me,
the violet-weaving Muses

## 74

And they made me famous
by the gift of their own work

## 75

THE EVENING STAR

Serenest of all stars

## 76

STAR OF EVENING

Hesperus
you bring
home everything
which light of day dispersed:
home the sheep herds
home the goat
home the mother's
darling

## 77

I SAID TO MY INSTRUMENT

Dumb tortoiseshell of mine
turn into a speaking thing divine

## 78

THE SLEEPY DOVES

Growing faint-headed
drop back their wings
and their hearts chill

**79**

And Through the Night Air
I heard the faint trickle
of the nymphs of the springs

---

### PLEASE

Come back to me, Gongyla, here tonight,
You, my rose, with your Lydian lyre.
There hovers forever around you delight:
    A beauty desired.

Even your garment plunders my eyes.
I am enchanted: I who once
Complained to the Cyrpus-born goddess,
    Whom now I beseech

Never to let this lose me grace
But rather bring you back to me:
Amongst all mortal women the one
    I most wish to see

# BOOK IV
## *Epithalamia*

### 81

YOU TOO, QUEEN

Auriferous Hecate
are lady-in-waiting to Aphrodite

### 82

THE HOMECOMING OF HECTOR AND ANDROMACHE

With power and speed in his legs came the herald,
Idaeus, announcing this wonderful news
    (Tidings that all over Asia
    Turned to a legend forever):
"Hector and all his companions are bringing
From sacred Thebe and the plains of Placia,
Over the salty sea by ship,
A delicate dark-eyed girl: Andromache.
    Many the golden bracelets
And purple stuffs the winds are bringing
      And trinkets bespangled;
Numberless too the silver cups and ivory chasings."

So uttered the herald, and Hector's dear father
    Nimbly arose as the news

Sped to their friends through the ample city.
    Then the people of Ilium
Harnessed their mules to the smoothly moving cars;
    And all the women in one,
    With the prettily ankled girls,
Ascended—the daughters of Priam apart.
    The men had the horses yoked
    To chariots; every youth
Was there: till a mighty people moved
     Mightly along.
    And the charioteers drove
    Their jingling horses on.


Then when Hector and Andromache
    Had mounted their car like gods,
    The great cavalcade set off
    And the city of people surged
     Back into Ilium
The honey-toned flute and the lyre were mixed
    With the click of the castanets.
    O, and the treble of girls—
     So holy and clear!
The dulcet echoes distilled to the sky
    Making Olympians laugh:
    And down all the streets there was mirth;
For the bowls and the cups were mixed, and from
    every shrine
  The cassia, myrrh, the frankincense curled.
    The older women as well
     Shouted their joy.
    And the men in a glorious paean
     Roared to Apollo—
That far-shooting god and lovely harper,
Singing aloud for the godlike pair:
    Hector and Andromache

---

### AS THE BRIDEGROOM SET OUT WE SANG

There
Stood
The mixing bowl mixed with ambrosia.
Hermes
Took
The ladle to pour out for the gods.
All
Then
Holding their goblets poured a libation:
So
Wished
The bridegroom the best of good luck

### 84

The cup was gold
with a twisted node

### 85

### I THOUGHT TO MYSELF

What are you like, gentle bridegroom, what?
Like a tender sapling, bridgegroom, *that.*

### WE SANG THE COUPLE TO THEIR HOME

Raise up the rafters high,
  Hurrah for the wedding!
Carpenters: higher and higher,
  Hurrah for the wedding!
The bridegroom is equal to Ares,
  Hurrah for the wedding!
Much taller than any tall man is,
  Hurrah for the wedding!
As tall as the singer of Lesbos,
  Hurrah for the wedding!
Towers over all singers of elsewhere,
  Hurrah for the wedding!

## 87

### WE PREPARED THE BRIDE

We swathed her in the softest cambric veil

## 88

O charming, O challenging lovely one!
Yours is to play with the rose-ankled Graces:
  yours to play with gold Aphrodite

## 89

Fashioned so beautifully, Bride!
There's honey in your eyes!
Your fair and love-strewn face . . .
Aphrodite, without doubt
has singled you out

## 90

### LUCKY

Bridegroom
there never was
another girl like this

## 91

"We shall give," said the father.

## 92

### THE PRIZE

BOYS' VOICES:   Like the last red apple
sweet and high:
High as the topmost twigs,
which the apple-pickers missed—
O no, not missed
but found beyond their fingertips

## THE PRICE

GIRLS' VOICES:  Like the mountain hyacinth
which feet of shepherds trample
leaving the ground in bloom
with blood of purple

### 93

I THINK

I shall be a maiden forever

### 94

Listen, my dear,
By the Goddess herself I swear
That *I* (like you)
Had only one
Virginity to spare
Yet did not fear
To go over the bridal line
When Hera bade me
And cast it from me;
So I cheer you on
and loudly declare:
"My own night was none
Too bad
And you my girl
Have nothing to fear,
Nothing at all."

---

## 95

### BRIDESMAIDS' CAROL

And all you maidens, prepare yourselves now
To sing through the night outside their door:
To sing of your love, groom, for your bride
  In her kirtle of violets.

So get yourselves up, girls, go hurry and fetch
The unmarried men, young as yourselves.
And let us all see as much sleep tonight
  As the lyre-voiced bird.*

## 96

### WE SANG OUTSIDE THEIR BEDCHAMBER

  Come, bride
  Brimming with roses
  Of love, bride,
  Gem of the lovely
  Goddess of Paphos:

  Go, bride,
  Go to the bed where
  Sweetly and gently
  You'll play with your bridegroom:

  So, bride,
  Hesperus lead you
  Star of the evening
  Happily onwards—
  Where you shall wonder,
  Where Hera on silver
  Sits Lady of Marriage

*The nightingale

## 97

OUTSIDE THEIR DOOR WE SHOUTED

The doorkeeper's feet
are seven fathoms deep:
His sandals take
twice five cobblers five
oxhides to make!

## 98

WHY AM I SAD?

Can it be I am thinking still
of my lost maidenhead?

## 99

WELL DONE!

Happiest bridegroom
Now that it's over:
Union you asked for,
Bride that you asked

## 100

Now go to sleep
on the breast of your sweetheart

———————

### 101

WE CALLED THROUGH THE KEYHOLE

Three cheers for the bride!
And bravo, you mettlesome bridegroom!

### 102

THEY WERE EXHAUSTED AND

The black trance of night
flooded into their eyes

### 103

OH!

Maidenhead! Maidenhead! where have you left me?
Gone and forever, Bride! Gone and forever!

104

BUT NOW

Let us go dear girls
Our carols are over,
For day is near

110

# BOOK V
## *The Taut Tongue*

### 105

#### LIVE YOUR OWN LIFE

As for the critic—
let brainstorms and maledictions sweep him away!

### 106

#### MY FINE GORGO

Many happy returns of the day
to the daughter of a great many kings!

### 107

#### BETWEEN YOU AND ME

We've had quite enough of Gorgo

## 108

### THOUGH

I'm not the spiteful sort at all
but have the spirit of a little child

## 109

### AND NOW

Love, thè limb-loosener, stirs me:
Irresistible, bitter-sweet imp.
But, Atthis, you've come to abhor me
(Even the hint of me)
And flit to Andromeda

## 110

### ANDROMEDA!

*She's* fired your fancy?
That clod of a woman
who hasn't even the knack
of pulling her skirts up
over her ankles

---

### III

**GO THEN**

You are nothing to me!

### 112

**WHO WANTS**

Love:
That weaver of yarns
Who gives presents of pain?

### 113

**THOUGH THEY SAY**

Love can make a poet out of a boor

### 114

**IT CAN OPEN THE EYES**

With the larkspur's stunning clarity

## 115

### LIKE JASON'S MANTLE

Mixed and parti-colored

## 116

### BUT EVEN THEN

I loved you, Atthis, long ago
my girlhood still in flowers . . . and you
A small ungainly girl, I thought

## 117

### I SAW LOVE

Come down from heaven
and fling off his purple cloak

## 118

### BUT I WON'T BE STUNG, SO

Keep your honey-bee
and keep your honey

## 119

### THEN APHRODITE SAID

All was not lost
When she forgot you
And fled to Andromeda.
O Sappho, of little faith!
I too have a right to scold you:
For you should have remembered
That wherever I was I loved you
And could have come from afar as before:
From Paphos, Panormus or Cyprus—
Where I am Queen and a mighty
Force for mankind, and for *you*:
A power like the blaze of the sun
Who lights up the world with his glory.
So remember that even in Acheron
I the love-enraveler
Can unravel the gloom. . . .
Yes, *I* can be with you.

---

## 120

### I AM GLAD TO SAY

Andromeda has been prettily paid back

## 121

### A REBUKE

ALCAEUS TO SAPPHO
Violet-decked, virtuous, honey-sweet smiling Sappho,
I've something to tell you but—ah!—shame stops me.
SAPPHO TO ALCAEUS
If you were after the good and the fair, sir,
And your tongue were not concocting a guilty message,
You wouldn't have shame in your eyes, sir,
    But say your say like an honest man.

## 122

### PROVERB

Fair is fair, young man, but only meets the eye.
Good is fair as well, or will be by and by.

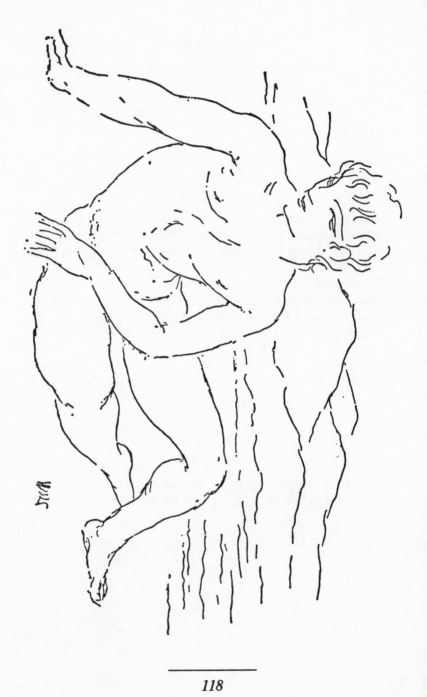

SO, YOU FINE YOUTH

Stand up and face me
friend to friend
Uncover me that charm
within your eyes

NO! IT WOULDN'T WORK

If you love me choose a younger
partner for your bed and board:
I could not bear to live, an elder
woman with a younger lord

THE LEAN MONTHS

Four months of continence—
Adonis inconsolate!

120

### HAVE THEM BOTH

Wealth without worth
is not a good companion:
put the two together
then you've top of fortune

### DON'T MALIGN IT

Gold is a child of Zeus
Gold is clean of rust
No worm nor weevil eats
Gold
It beats
The strongest human wits

### YET, FOR ALL YOUR WEALTH

Dead, you'll lie there, woman, unregarded:
No one to recall you ever after
You who had no share
Of the roses from Pieria.
Feeble in the cellars of Lord Death,
Obscure even there,
You'll flit among uncelebrated dead

---

### 129

Forgotten—
Loathsome and incongruous word
To all the Muses of Pieria

### 130

#### IN EXILE

O Peace!
I've never found you quite so boring yet

### 131

#### BEFORE THEY HAD THEIR BROOD

Leto and Niobe
were the closest of cronies

### 132

#### A PRETTY THING

But need you be
quite so proud
of a ring?

### YOUR HAIR NEEDS NOTHING, MY GIRL

My mother would say that when she was young
Nothing could touch a crimson band

Looped through the hair—and no denying—
But a girl with hair like a fall of flame

Couldn't do better than a crown of flowers. . . .
Anyway, Cleïs, I don't have a thing

Like a gorgeous Sardian headband now
And not the slightest idea of where

(With the Cleanax clan controlling town)
A gorgeous headband can be found. . . .

Of course our Mytilenan remnants are
All rotted away

### I DO PRAY FOR CHARAXUS

Golden Nereids, please may my brother return here
Safely; please may all his heart's desires be
Amply accomplished.

Also, may his former transgressions all be
Paid for; he become a delight to us his
Dear ones, a pain to his enemies—not to
Any of us. O

Make him want to honor his sister. Let me
Not remember bitterly words with which he
Tried to hurt me—O my rubuke had rankled!—
Before he departed.

Ah, and when he does in the end come back here,
Make him cut adrift from his riotous comrades.
Then if he really wants it, take to a decent girl
    And honorably marry her


## 135

### VERY WELL, CHARAXUS

If you must flutter around the steps of the great and
Not of the noble and true, and say good-bye to
All your friends and get so swollen-headed
    You hurt me and say I am

Only a nuisance—well, enjoy it up to the
Hilt; but I am not soft-minded enough to
    Pay attention to childish tantrums.

Make no mistake, for the trick won't catch an
Old bird who has put two and two together and
Understands to the core the cad you were before
    And what she is up against.

Better reform and take advice, for I know
*I* am not a difficult person, so have
    On *my* side the angels


## 136

### THE BOASTER

Ares, of course,
says he can drag off
Hephaestus
by sheer force

---

## 137

### THEY SAY

No one can count
the cups you quaff

## 138

### I HOPE DORICHA LEARNS HER LESSON

Cypris, let her discover
that even *you* have gone a little bit sour
now that people are jeering:
"My, what an excellent catch
is Doricha's second"

## 139

### I SHAN'T MENTION THAT PERSON, CHARAXUS

With whom you are locked in vagabond love,
supposing that to be beautiful
which is public property

## 140

Oh yes, it is all quite plain to me.

### 141

#### OH, IF ONE CAN

When rage flares up inside the heart
Lock up the tongue with its useless bark


### 142

#### BEACH SMELLS?

Don't poke among the pebbles

# BOOK VI

## *Memory and Valediction*

### 143

Yes
they gave me
true success
the golden
Muses
And once dead
I shall not be forgotten

### 144

Many have been cheated by oblivion
But by good judges
None:
And afterwards, I say,
I shall be remembered
Certainly by some

---

## 145

### THEY WERE GOING

And I said to them: "Sweet women
how you will remember always
till you are old
the things we did together
in shining youth!
For many the things we did then
innocent and beautiful
And now that you go from here
my heart is breaking

## 146

### I LOVED IT

When the gentle feet of the Cretan girls
Danced in tune round some intimate shrine
Treading the smooth soft bloom of the lawn

## 147

And the moon rose clear and full
On girls grouped round the altar

---

## 148

### I REMEMBER

That night of ours.
O, I can tell you
I begged it could be doubled

## 149

### I SEE IT STILL AND FEEL IT: THE

. . . passion, yes
. . . utterly
. . . I can.
. . . shall be to me
. . . a face
. . . shining back at me
. . . beautiful
. . . indelibly

### DO YOU RECALL THE MORNING LETTER YOU
### ONCE SENT ME:

"Sappho, I swear if you don't come out I'll hate you!
Do get up for the love of us all and shake your
Beautiful energy free from bed; as sweet as
A lily beside a pool at dawn drop off your
Nightgown from Chios, bathe in the water; and Cleïs
Shall fetch you your saffron blouse out from the wood-
    chest
And your purple dress, wrap a peignoir around you,
Bind in your hair blossomy fillets to crown you.
Come, darling, with all that beauty of yours that makes
    me
Mad! I shall ask Praxinoa to roast some chestnuts,
And *I* shall prepare the girls a grandlier breakfast.
One of the gods, my dear chickabiddy, has blessed us.
This is the day that Sappho—loveliest lady—
Has promised to bring herself back to Mytilene
(Friendliest city)—together with us go back there
A mother among her own children." . . . Dear Atthis,
O tell me, have you forgotten all this that happened
    Such ages ago? Or do you remember?

151

### AND ONCE I USED TO CALL OUT

Long life and health—for me—
No wrinkles, children . . . Youth!

Ah, if my breasts could still give suck
And my womb bear a child, wouldn't I come
Quickly without a qualm to another
    Bridegroom and bed!

Innumerable now are the wrinkles spread
Across my flesh by age, and Love
Does not fly to me, chase me, give me again
    His beautiful pain

## 153

### AN ETERNAL CRY

GIRLS' VOICES:   He is dying, Cythereia, dying,
    the delicate Adonis:
    what can we do?
BOYS' VOICES:   O batter your breasts, young girls,
    and tear your dress into tatters

## 154

### YET I TOO ONCE COULD EXCLAIM

Mother dear, I cannot mind my loom
And Aphrodite is to blame:
    I'm almost dead
    with love-longing for a stripling lad

---

## 155

### BUT AT THIS SEASON

Why does that daughter of Pandion
the high-flying swallow
come to molest me?

## 156

### I AM AS LIMP AS

a wet worn-out dishcloth

## 157

### I WHO ONCE WAS

Minister to the Cyprus-born
the wily Aphrodite

### LET'S NOT PRETEND

No, Children, do not delude me.
You mock the good gifts of the Muses
When you say: "Dear Sappho we'll crown you,
Resonant player,
First on the clear sweet lyre. . . ."
Do you not see how I alter:
My skin with its aging,
My black hair gone white,
My legs scarcely carrying
Me, who went dancing
More neatly than fawns once
(Neatest of creatures)?
No, no one can cure it; keep beauty from going,
And *I* cannot help it.
God himself cannot do what cannot be done.
So age follows after and catches
Everything living.
Even rosy-armed Eos, the Dawn,
Who ushers in morning to the ends of the earth,
Could not save from the grasp of old age
Her lover immortal Tithonus.
And I too, I know, must waste away.
Yet for me—listen well—
My delight is the exquisite.
Yes, for me,
Glitter and sunlight and love
Are one society.
So I shall not go creeping away
To die in the dark:
I shall go on living with you,
Loving and loved.

## 159

### BELIEVE ME

Death is an evil:
The gods think so
Or would have died—
O long ago!

## 160

### BUT REST ASSURED

Towards you pretty ones
this mind of mine
can never change

## 161

So long as you wish it

ON THE BASE OF THE STATUE WERE THE WORDS

"Only a baby girl, not able to talk yet,
But ask me a question and I shall tell you
With the voice that is always at my feet:
'A present to fiery Aethopia, Leto's child,
From Aristo, daughter of Hermocleitus
(Son of Saunaïdas), priestess of yours,
O Lady of ladies! Be kind and thank us,
Giving our family fame' "

163

WE SENT HER HOME WITH THESE WORDS ON THE URN

"This is the dust of poor little Timas
dead before she was wed
Whom Persephone took to her somber chamber:
for whose demise so far from home
all her tender companions sheared
with keen new blades
the lovely hair from their heads"

164

Alone of the gods, Hades
sanctions no measure
of sweet hope.

---

## 165

**I SAW ON A TOMBSTONE BY THE SEA**

"To Pelagon the fisherman
Meniscus his father
puts this basket up and oar blade
in memory
of a life that was difficult"

## 166

**I THINK OF ACHILLES**

He lies
in the black earth at last
at the end of his toils.
Oh what suffering was brought to pass
by the sons of Atreus!

## 167

The understanding gods evoke tears

### DEATH SEEMED TO BECKON

Then Gongyla spoke: ". . . You cannot be sure—
Or have your eyes seen a sign?" "They have,"
I said, "for Hermes has come in a dream.
'Master,' I said, 'I am lost.
By Juno the Holy, I swear
I no longer care
for success:
I wish
I could die . . . I wish,
I could see the dew
on the lotus banks of Acheron' "

### AND HERMES REPLIED

And yet great glory
will come on you
in every place where Phaëthon shines—
even in the halls
of Acheron

### NEVERTHELESS, CLEÏS

The sounds of mourning do not suit
a house which serves the Muse:
they are not wanted here

LIFE SLIPS BY

The moon has gone
The Pleiades gone
In dead of night
Time passes on
I lie alone

# APPENDIX

## Some Notes on the Dilemma of Translating Sappho

LONGINUS IN HIS treatise *On the Sublime* talks of Sappho's style as γλαφυρὰ καὶ ανθηρὰ σύνθε σις—which one might translate as "a smooth and colorful style" or "a polished and florescent style." Haines calls it "easy, graceful, pointed, direct, and simple—simple above all." Curiously he omits in this list the most obvious attribute of all: "musical." And that is where the trouble begins. What does one do about the music? It is not merely that Sappho's poems were accompanied by music (on one or more of the stringed instruments for which Lesbos was famous) but that the poems themselves—the actual words spoken or chanted—are rigorously organized into patterns of sound. They have an επιφώνημα, a kind of vocal epiphany, as Demetrius (contemporary of Cicero) calls it in his work *On Harmony*. Plutarch, too, more than once mentions the immediate effect she has upon listeners: "Do you not see what a charm there is in Sappho's songs," he says, "and how they delight and tickle the ears . . . ?" There is no getting away from the fact that the verbal music of Sappho is as catchy and lively as "hit tunes." Is one to ignore it? That is the question. Is the limpid clarity of the image the main thing and—when it comes to translating—all else ornamental flourish?

To be able to think so would make the problem infinitely easier. It would line it up immediately with much that is most modern in our poetic tradition. One could at once go ahead (with one's ear as a sleeping partner) and treat Sappho as if she were Chinese. The results would have all the virtues of the acceptably best way of translating Chinese. It would be easy to read, it would be exact and compressed, it would seem modern. Best of all, it would not be in the least contrived. It would be "easy, graceful, pointed, direct, and simple—simple above all." But would it be Sappho? No, it would not. Or shall we say: it would be only *half* Sappho. The other half would be obliterated.

Even if one cheats a little and divides up the lines into formal syllabic patterns to look like verse, it still will not be Sappho. Syllabic poetry of this kind, in which crystal-clear prose is divided up into lines and stanzas by a regular count of syllables, has nothing to do with sonic stress and rhythm. A fortiori, it has nothing to do with Greek prosody, which does indeed count the syllables but only as a means of establishing fixed and unmistakable audial quantities that actually can be heard—not merely detected with the mind. Such a system has very little to do with English poetry either, whose genius I believe to be accentual—the genius in fact of the nursery rhymes in Mother Goose— where the count of the syllables is unimportant and only the count of the stresses matters.

But even this is only half of half-a-story. So far we have talked only about rhythm. What about the actual sound: the sound of the vowels and the sound of the consonants? Can we ignore the richly inlaid sonic gems with which every line of Sappho sparkles? I mean the alliteration, the assonance, the consonance—yes, and even the rhyme—all that cross-linking throughout of every kind of sonal analogy. The truth of the matter is that whatever the secret of Sappho's poetry the one thing that it is *not* is simple—least of all "simple above all." What it does is to give the *illusion* of being simple, and it is precisely the effort to reproduce this illusion together with the beauty of the music that we are asking ourselves if we can make.

The illusion flows preeminently from sound and sense working together and yet almost independently. The sense of the lines is natural, graceful, effortless, and direct. Their sound—the actual music of the prosody—is consummately contrived and subtle. The sense is idiomatic, unliterary, and often very near the colloquial. Indeed the language is Sappho's own Aeolic Lesbian dialect, which does not eschew the cliché or the conventional epithet where this is right for both the music and the effect of naturalness. The *sound*, again, is formal, calculated, and strictly ordered. In brief, it looks as if Sappho's poetry is, of all extant poetries, the most unlike (and equally unlike), both the Romantic flourishes of the pre-Georgians *and* the purist, Imagist tradition of the last seventy years which has all but done away with the boundaries between poetry and prose. We need not here bother with the first: no one in this day and age is going to make her into a Romantic . . . but we do need to be on our guard against the second, against treating Sappho as an Imagist.

What emerges rather surprisingly from a detached observance of her style--a surprise which I imagine will come as a shock to many moderns—is that, in the Poundian sense, it by no means excludes "bad writing": that is, writing which for all its concision and exactness does often generalize, repeat, tautologize, and is as much interested in engendering feeling through the quality of sheer incantation as in giving information. If one were pushed to make a choice, I should say that it is more like Heine than the Imagists, more like Swinburne than Eliot. One might not even be absolutely wrong in saying that, given tradition for tradition—the Classical for the Romantic—it contains a proportion of verbal redundancies for the sake of musical feeling at least half as high as any "Solitary Reaper" or *Rime of the Ancient Mariner*. Even in the ποικιλόθρον ἀθάνατ' Αφρόδιτα, *Call to Aphrodite*

("Undying and dapple-throned Aphrodite," as I have translated it in my third version in the Notes), one of the most intricately knit of all Sappho's love songs and her acknowledged masterpiece, there are instances of it: charm of sound taking precedence over exactitude of information. She does not, in other words, when she comes to writing poetry, play Robert Graves's game of "telegrams": cutting out every word which is not immediately required by the sense. For instance, in the third line of ποικιλόθρον we have μὴ μ' ἄσαισι μηδ' ονίαισι δάμνα, which in the purist view would have to be regarded as containing tautology, for ἄσαισι and ονίαισι mean virtually the same thing: "suffering and sorrow." Yet it is precisely this choice of words which gives Sappho the opportunity of five splendid alliterations and one internal rhyme, making this one of the unforgettable lines in Greek literature. Again in the tenth line of the same poem we have γαν μέλαιναν "black earth": nothing more than a stock epithet, but it enables her to echo the assonances in κάλω and σ' αγον of the line before and delicately to hit again the sound of the gamma. Then, in the last stanza, there is the redundancy of χαλέπαν μερίμναν, "harsh trouble," and also perhaps of θῦμος ιμμέρει, "desire (heart) wants," which is a near chiché. All these "infidelities" make an unforgettably telling and beautiful impact on the ear, proving to our generation (I hope) what it has yet to discover; that "bad writing" in the prose way is not necessarily bad poetry. For if the function of poetry is to lead to emotive response by way of the senses and feeling—and only thus to the intellect—and if it is true that music reaches the senses and the heart more immediately than any prose sense can do, and if in fact pure music does not have any meaning at all in the conceptual order of prose sense, and if finally "melopoeia" is one of the essential aspects of verbal music—then it must surely follow that a "poetry" which hews too directly to the line of sense instead of to the line of sound and sensation is in fact thwarting one half its purpse. The most exact information in the world is slower in getting to the heart than music is. Indeed, the rigorous adhering to the exactest way of giving the sense can obliterate the power of the words as sounds. Besides, if seemingly "bad writing"— imprecisions, woolly words, abstractions—are ostracized, not only is the sonic verbal scale seriously impaired but all chance is taken away of the subconscious ear remaining subconscious, since the intellect is then called upon to do a full-time job of attending to meanings. I believe it is actually against the nature of memorable lyric poetry to limit itself to words which force the conscious mind to remain conscious. Such is precisely the function of prose.

The genius of Sappho is that she keeps a miraculous balance: a balance between sound and sense, between verbal uselessness-for-the-sake-of-sound and verbal precision for the sake of sense. Nine-tenths of the time she manages to give the impression of incredible economy—which is also real. She is as clear as a mountain spring and as swift as clean water running over tinted pebbles. One might say that she is also as hard and clear-edged as marble, but this too is partly illusion. She wrote in fact in the softest of all Greek dialects—not at all the crystalline and finely chiseled Attic Greek of two centuries later—and her imagery is rich and sensuous. Half the secret, I believe—apart from the fact that Greek is an inflected language and therefore is able to be direct even when the music becomes intricate—lies in the actual tempo. It takes appreciably less time to pronounce eleven syllables of Greek than eleven syllables of English; that is, if all the syllables in the English are actually sounded. This is not just because the vowels in the Greek are often shorter but that the English tends to use twice or thrice as many consonants (and consonants delay). The thing can be proved quite easily by taking any line of Sappho's and writing it out in separate syllables with experimental English equivalents written underneath. Take for instance the line: Χρύσιαι Νηρήιδες ἀβλάβην μοι and write out underneath each syllable of it: *Góldĕn Nérĕĭds, pléase măy my bróthĕr sáfelў.* Here you have the same number of syllables in each (eleven), the same meter (Sapphic), and yet the English comes out appreciably longer. There are four words in Greek, eight in the English; eleven consonants in the Greek, twenty-one in the English. This is typical. The only way of keeping eleven syllables in the English, should one want to (and it is by no means necessary since the number of *stresses* not syllables is what counts in the English), and still making it sonically more or less equal to the Greek, is to increase the tempo of the English by giving it a different rhythm: a rhythm in fact where some of the syllables are scarcely sounded. Such a sentence might be: *Gōldĕn Nérĕĭds, rĕtúrn mĕ mў bróthĕr.* Here the important thing is not that the same number of syllables has been kept but that a whole metrical foot has been chopped off the line, that the English tempo is now esthetically equivalent to the Greek, and that the remaining trochees and dactyls are still able (or rather are able for the first time) to give the *illusion* of Sapphic meter.

The corollary of such a discovery is of tremendous importance to the poet-translator: namely that the exact imitating of the outward form of Greek poetry, so far from being nearer to the original esthetically, can very easily be further away. . . . Oh, the thing can be done. Swinburne, Professor Lattimore, and many others have shown what *can* be done, but, except in the greatest hands, the effort is liable to end in a considerable disservice to one's own language, forcing it to strain at exactly the point where it ought to give the impression of being most itself and most at ease. Even Swinburne's Sapphics, beautiful though they are, are appreciably longer in each line than anything in Sappho and are by no means the esthetic equivalent.

An example of the sort of dilemma a translator faces is seen in No. 171. Here is the passage in Sappho's Greek:

> Δέδυκε μὲν ἀ σέλαννα
> καὶ Πληΐαδες, μέσαι δὲ
> νύκτες, παρὰ δ᾽ ἔρχετ᾽ ὥρα,
> ἔγω δὲ μόνα κατεύδω.

Here is the same passage put into phonetic English with the Greek natural stresses marked:

Dédŭkĕ mén ăh sĕlánă
kai Pleiiádĕs mĕsáidĕ
nŭktés pără dérkĕt óră
égŏ dĕ mónă kătĕudŏ.

Now let us see what happens if we translate the Greek in a way to reproduce as much as possible of Sappho's meter, keeping to her eight syllables per line. We get something like the following:

The moon has set and the Pleiads,
Far gone is the night and the hours
Pass on their way; I am left here
Lying, oh so very alone!

Note first of all that though the Greek prosodically is composed of three metrical feet and is equivalent to four stresses, in fact, if the natural value of syllables is sounded instead of the theoretical quantities, it is equivalent to three stresses: (see next chapter on a New Approach to Greek Meters). All this is reproduced fairly faithfully in the English version. We now have Sappho's meter but surely something has gone wrong with the whole feel of the Greek. We have lost Sappho's economy, precision, starkness. The verse trips merrily on the tongue like a dance measure. Although the number of syllables in the Greek and English is the same, Sappho uses only sixteen words to the English twenty-eight, and only thirty-four consonants to the English sixty. Paradoxically, by sticking close to the Greek prosody we have got very far away from the aesthetic equivalent, which, I submit, is much more nearly matched in my original version.

The moon has gone
The Pleiades gone
In dead of night
Time passes on
I lie alone

Is there any answer, then, to the impossible problem of translating Sappho? All poetry, of course, is impossible to translate—a truism one gets tired of hearing—but Sappho seems to be more difficult to handle than any Greek poet except perhaps Pindar. She is infinitely harder to capture than Aeschylus, Sophocles, and Euripides—even in their choruses. If there is a partial answer to the challenge, it seems to me that it must be along the lines I have outlined: the lines of *illusion*—a very different thing from the two easy ways out: bastard Chinese or pseudo-Swinburnian. There seems to be no other way of trying to face both directions at once: of being direct, clear, precise, natural, and simple above all, yet at the same moment polished, colorful, subtle, and in the musical form which, though calculated and ordered, is immediate and recognizable.

Meanwhile, there *is* a way of shortening the Greek line in English even while keeping to the essence of the Greek measure, thus bringing the tempos of the two poetries together. In my own translations I have not always done this—for English on occasion has a right to be longer than the Greek—but the technique evolved was often an immense help to me in trying to decide the great dilemma which forever remains: how to re-create the magic, by creating the illusion, of that unmistakable essence which is Sappho.

# Greek Meters
# Outline to a New Approach

SO MUCH HAS been written on Greek meters that the systems and counter systems of interpretation which have been evolved, the pronunciamentos that have been made, and the plain obfuscation that has resulted would daunt a genius. One would not deny that Greek prosody is complex, varied, and as rich as the language itself, but that it is incomprehensible to the ears of human beings who live in a different age is, I firmly believe, a machination of grammarians. Things are simpler and also more natural than has been made out.

To begin with, every student knows that "Greek metric is not accentual, but quantitative. That is to say, the rhythm is based on units in which the balance of syllables is dictated not by the loudness, or stress, with which it is spoken, but by quantity, or the time taken to speak it."[1] In other words, Greek vowels have well-defined quantities, long or short, which are largely lacking in modern European languages, so that when we read them we have to replace long by stressed and short by unstressed.

This is the accepted view, but it has been so overemphasized that, for all practical purposes, it leaves the heart of the matter out. What nobody seems to have noticed is that the two schemes of metric, quantity and stress, do *not* in fact run counter to each

[1]C. M. Bowra, *The Greek Experience*. New York: The World Publishing Company, 1957; The New American Library (Mentor Books), 1959.

other, but parallel, and possess between them a per-
fect analogy of metric. What has been left out is this:
the fact that Greek and English share (on top of their
metrical heritages) a treasury of spoken rhythms where
quantity and stress become almost interchangeable
terms. Crystallized into principles it amounts to this.
In Greek you have schemes of quantitative rhythm
which cut across the natural accents or stress values of
words. In English you have schemes of stress rhythm
which cut across the natural accents or stress values of
words. The difference is that in English the stress
value of the syllables is not constant, whereas in Greek
the quantitative value of the syllables (within certain
limits) *is*. Take these lines:

> Híckĕrў díckĕrў dóck
> Thĕ móuse răn úp thĕ clóck
> Thĕ clóck strúck óne
> Thĕ móuse răn dówn
> Híckĕrў díckĕrў dóck

Here the stress value of the vowels is liable to shift
according to the position of the word in the line. For
instance, *ran* in line 2 is unstressed and equivalent to
short, but stressed and equivalent to long in line 4. If I
alter the meter (which here is three-stress rhythm) into
iambic tetrameter, but use the very same words and
write:

> Thĕ móuse thăt rán, răn úp thĕ clóck
> Thĕ clóck strúck óne, thĕ móuse răn dówn
> Thĕ clóck. Ŏ híckĕrў́! Ŏ dóck!

*ran* becomes once stressed and equivalent to long, and
twice unstressed and equivalent to short. *Struck* be-
comes unstressed and short. The *y* of *hickery* becomes

---

stressed and long. All this notwithstanding the fact that in speech rhythm *ran* would normally be stressed rather than *up, struck* would not go unstressed, and the *y* at the end of *hickery* could not be anything but short. It is clear then that meter can reverse the natural values of speech rhythm. An even more obvious example is the single line:

The bŏy stoŏd ón thĕ búrnĭng déck

Here, *stood*, long by nature, is made short by meter.[2] And *on*, short by nature, is made long by meter. There are, in other words, two rhythms operative at once: that of natural speech and that of meter—often hitting on opposed stresses yet coinciding enough to make a fusion of the two within the line. Which rhythm is allowed to predominate depends on the individual sensitivity of the reader. One approximates to the quality of music, the other to that of speech.

I believe very much the same happens in Greek; except that here instead of the stresses being fixed by meter they are fixed by the invariable quantities of the vowels themselves. One might say that in English the syllables change their time values to accommodate the metrical stresses, whereas in Greek the stresses change their time pattern to accommodate the fixed values of the syllables. The important thing—the thing precisely which makes the two metrics share an analogy—is that Greek too possesses a natural heritage of speech rhythms which cut across or are cut across by the metrical structure—be it of quantity or stress. The theorists seem to have supposed that because stress is arrived at in English prosody by meter, and in Greek by quantity, natural word accent is important in En-

[2]I do not mean that one would necessarily scan it like this but that this is the theoretical meter: this is the underlying regularity against which the variations are counterpointed.

glish but of no importance in Greek.[3] This is an unwarranted assumption: arbitrary and unnatural.[4]

My conclusions then are these: in Greek and English (and probably in all poetries) there are two sets of sonic principles operating at once: the rhythm set up by the meter or the arrangement of fixed quantities, and the rhythm set up by the natural time values of speech. Either set of principles can be given the supremacy. If overwhelmingly the first, we get incantation. If overwhelmingly the second, we get no meter at all and only such emotions as can be squeezed out of prose. The art of reading poetry is to use the natural speech values as a foil to the metrical, and play them off as counterpoint; always leaving enough of the meter to keep it a foil and never letting the counterpoint take over. Therefore we do not say:

The bóy stoŏd ón thĕ búrniñg déck

though the theoretical meter requires it, but:

The bóy stóod oñ thĕ búrniñg déck.

And we do not say with Sappho:

[3]Professor D. S. Raven's proof of this is invalid. He says: ". . . while there is a close correspondence in the quantity between strophe and antistrophe (in the Greek choruses) there is no similar correspondence in word accent." Of course not! Why should there be? There is no correspondence in word accent between any two lines of "The Boy Stood on the Burning Deck"!

[4]There is a coda to this that also needs to be quashed. It is often suggested that we do not know what classical Greek sounded like. This is utterly misleading. We do not one hundred percent know what it sounded like—yes. We do not know essentially what it sounded like—nonsense. We know what the stresses were, we know the possible variations of pronunciation: the language remains equally beautiful in any of them. If this were not true, there would be little point to our studies. What value has this incredible poetry, what equipment for conjuring up feeling and passion, if it is to be reduced simply to a poetry of content—of information unrelated to sound? We do not read the Greek language for the hieroglyphic beauty of its characters.

$$\bar{\text{O}}\iota\ \breve{\mu}\epsilon\nu\ \bar{\iota}\pi\pi\eta\omega\nu\ \sigma\tau\rho\sigma\tau\sigma\nu\ \bar{o}\iota\ \delta\epsilon\ \pi\epsilon\sigma\delta\omega\nu$$

oi men ippeon stroton oi de pesdon

though the meter requires it, but with Sappho:

$$\bar{\text{O}}\iota\ \breve{\mu}\epsilon\nu\ \bar{\iota}\pi\pi\eta\omega\nu\ \sigma\tau\rho\sigma\tau\sigma\nu\ \bar{o}\iota\ \delta\epsilon\ \pi\epsilon\sigma\delta\omega\nu$$

oi men ippeon stroton oi de pesdon

In either case, what emerges from the tension between the two sets of values is a new music based on both.

## Basic Feet in Greek Poetry

| | |
|---|---|
| ⌣ ‒ | iamb |
| ‒ ⌣ | trochee |
| ⌣ ⌣ ‒ | anapaest |
| ‒ ⌣ ⌣ | dactyl |
| ‒ ⌣ ‒ | cretic |
| ⌣ ‒ ‒ | bacchius |
| ⌣ ⌣ ‒ ‒ | ionic |
| ‒ ⌣ ⌣ ‒ | choriamb |
| ‒ ⌣ ‒ ‒ | epitrite |
| ⌣ ‒ ‒ ⌣ ‒ | dochmius |
| ‒ ‒ | spondee[5] |

[5]Not strictly the basis of any meter, but found as an ingredient in other meters.

# Principal Meters Used by Sappho

— ᵛ — ᵛ — ᵛ —                                Glyconic
— ᵛ — ᵛ ᵛ — ᵛ — —                            hendecasyllable (Glyconic
                                             with addition of ᵛ — — )
— ᵛ — — — ᵛ ᵛ — ᵛ — —   thrice              Sapphic stanza
— ᵛ ᵛ — —   4th line

— ᵛ — ᵛ ᵛ — ᵛ ᵛ — ᵛ — ᵛ —                    Sapphic-14-syllable
— ᵛ — ᵛ — — ᵛ ᵛ — — ᵛ ᵛ — —                  Sapphic-16-syllable
ᵛ ᵛ — — ᵛ ᵛ — —                              minor Ionic
ᵛ — ᵛ ᵛ — — ᵛ ᵛ — — ᵛ ᵛ — —                  major Ionic
ᵛ ᵛ — ᵛ — ᵛ — —                              Anacreontic (a rearranged
                                             Ionic)
≡ ᵛ ᵛ ≡ ᵛ ᵛ ≡                                choriambic dimeter
— ᵛ ᵛ — ᵛ ᵛ — ᵛ ᵛ — ᵛ ᵛ — ᵛ ᵛ — ᵛ          dactylic hexameter
— ᵛ ᵛ — ᵛ ᵛ — ᵛ ᵛ — ᵛ ᵛ — ᵛ                 dactylic pentameter
— ᵛ ᵛ — ᵛ ᵛ — ᵛ ᵛ — ᵛ                        dactylic tetrameter
                                             elegiac
dactylic hexameter
followed by  — ᵛ ᵛ — ᵛ ᵛ —|—ᵛ ᵛ — ᵛ ᵛ —

ᵛ — ᵛ — ᵛ — ᵛ ᵛ — ᵛ —
ᵛ — ᵛ — ᵛ — ᵛ ᵛ — ᵛ   twice              Alcaic stanza

— ᵛ ᵛ — ᵛ ᵛ — ᵛ — —

(i) The Aeolic base is any one of these couples ᵛ ᵛ / — — / — ᵛ. The following meters use it for their first two syllables as an alternative to — ᵛ: Glyconic, hendecasyllable, Sapphic-14 and 16-syllable, dactylic pentameter and tetrameter, and major Ionic.

(ii) Aeolic meter includes all those meters which have both the sequences — ᵛ — and — ᵛ ᵛ —. The so-called major Ionic is therefore included, but not true dactylic meter or elegiacs or minor Ionic. Dactylic meters normally have the final syllable - or ᵛ.

(iii) Feet are not usually marked off now, because they are not regarded as a real unit. Glyconics, for example, are analyzed into these units: Aeolic base plus choriamb plus iamb.

## Greek Meters Transposed
## into English Stress Rhythms[6]

Glyconic:

"Nó," she sáid, "or I'll téll my múm."

Hendecasyllable:

"Nó," she sáid, "or I'll téll my múm at ónce. Gó."

Sapphic stanza:

Cóme, my lóve, to whére I can gáze upón you.

Dón't you knów that áll little girls adóre you?

Dón't you knów that húngrily théy will eát you?

Dón't be a fóol, lóve!

Sapphic-14-syllable:

Ónce a beáutiful Húguenot wént to the tówn of Róme.

Sapphic-16-syllable:

Péople néver belíeve pípes in the cóld winter can fréeze and búrst.

Minor Ionic:

To suggést múrder is wróng, sír.

Major Ionic:

Good-býe then untíl Márch the eléventh, noón, in the Pláza Pálm Róom.

Anacreontic:

In the spríng of Eíghty-twó, déar.

---

[6]Having in mind that in English the accent often falls dubiously and hesitantly and the rhythm remains uncertain, whereas in Greek the vowels have fixed quantities and the rhythm is perfectly emphatic from the start.

---

Choriambic dimeter:

Óh that I máy! Óh that I máy!

Dactylic hexameter:

Bréak with the séas and the téaring of wínds over
sílvery lándscapes.

Dactylic pentameter:

Bréak with the séas and the téaring of wínds over
rámparts.

Bréak with the séas in the ráge of the wínter.

Dactytic tetrameter:

Bréak with the séas in the ráge of the wínter.

Elegiac:

Thís is the rúinous státe revolútion has fórced on the
nátion.

Thése are the áshes of what ónce was a próud little
ísle.

Alcaic stanza:

There's nóthing yóu not Í nor a síngle sóul
Wánts móre than lóve and fáme and a líttle pówer.
We múst be wánted, múst be nóted,
Múst have a pláce in the thóught of mánkind.

# Important Events Before, During, and After Sappho

| | |
|---|---|
| 776 B.C. | First Olympic Games |
| 750–700 C. | Homer & Hesiod |
| 620 | Beginnings of Greek philosophy in Miletus, the capital city of Ionia in Asia Minor |
| 620–570 | Conflict between Lesbos and the Athenian colony of Sigeum in Asia Minor (where many battles of the Trojan War were fought and where Achilles was buried) |
| 615 | The prophet Nahum prophesies the destruction of Nineveh, capital of the Assyrian Empire |
| 612 | Babylonians under Nabopolassar take Nineveh |
| 608 | Jeremiah prophesies the destruction of Jerusalem |
| 605 | Nebuchadnezzar is master of Babylonia and Judah |
| 597 | Nebuchadnezzar crushes Judean rebellion. Mass transportation of Jews to Babylon (first Babylonian captivity). |
| 594 | Solon, statesman and poet, codifies Athenian laws and lays the foundations of democracy |
| 593 | Prophecies of Ezekiel in Nineveh |
| 586 | Nebuchadnezzar crushes Judean revolt and destroys the Temple in Jerusalem (second Babylonian captivity). |
| 580 C. | Birth of Pythagoras |
| 563 | Birth of Buddha |
| 556 | Birth of Simonides |
| 551 | Birth of Confucius |

| | |
|---|---|
| 550 | Croesus becomes king of Lydia (opposite Lesbos) and the richest man in the world |
| 538 | Cyrus takes Babylon. The end of the Babylonian Empire and the beginning of the Persian. End of the Babylonian captivity. |
| 509 | Foundation of the Roman Republic |
| 490 | Athenian defeat of the Persians at Marathon |
| 483 | Birth of Herodotus |
| 480 | Persians defeated at the naval battle of Salamis and Greece saved. |
| 471 | Birth of Thucydides |
| 525–385 | The greatest period of Greek drama: Aeschylus, Sophocles, Euripides, Aristophanes |
| 469 | Birth of Socrates |

# Notes

*The Greek text I have used is based on that edited by J. M. Edmonds in the Loeb Classical Library, with emendations from Page, Haines, Hills, and others, (and in a few instances my own). Translations of Greek source notes which I quote from the Loeb are for the most part new translations which I have made* ad hoc. Edm. followed by a number indicates the number of the poem or fragment in Edmonds. Where a text is not given by Edmonds I have gone direct to the latest Oxyrhynchus Papyrus or other source as published by Campbell.

## *1*

Edm.1a. Meter doubtful.
Taken from a late fifth-century painting on the three-handled damaged hydria in the Athens Museum. The words, uncertainly decipherable, are visible on the scroll which Sappho is unrolling. The scroll is entitled ῎Επεα πτερόεντα, or Winged Words. Their genuineness is doubted by some. See Haines #48/5 and plate XII.

1: From a reference in a letter of the Emperor Julian it appears possible that Sappho placed these words (one line in the Greek) at the head of her own collection of her poems.

2: Libraries are known to have been collected in Sappho's day by Polycrates of Samos and Pisistratus of Athens. Weigall writes:

Sappho doubtless possessed an extensive library, the books—that is to say, scrolls—being kept in chests divided for the purpose into pigeon holes; and since many modern writers seem to question the use of such scrolls in her time I must draw attention to the fact that Herodotus expressly refers to scrolls of papyrus or parchment as having been introduced before this period into Greece by way of Ionia,* as of course anybody might have guessed, since papyrus had already been in use in Egypt for two thousand years, and Egypt had been in touch with the Greek world for centuries. The Greeks, I may mention, rendered the Egyptian word for papyrus scroll as "biblos," whence came their word "biblion," a "book," from which our word "bible" and compounds such as "bibliography" are derived.†

Donald Lucas comments:

Libraries on any scale were not widely available before the late fifth century. Polycrates and Pisistratus had some rolls, Euripides may have had quite a collection. How Sappho kept her scrolls no one knows. . . . Egypt was not continuously in touch with the Greek world after the Mycenaean Age and Herodotus does not tell us how long before his time papyrus came into use. In Sappho's day it was probably fairly recent.

**2**

Edm.12. Meter, Sapphic.
Quoted by Athenæus (writing in the first half of the third century A.D.), *Doctors at Dinner*, to show that there is not necessarily any reproach in the use of the word ἑταίρα or "comrade." Sappho calls her young companions "hetairai" with perfect innocence, though later the word came to denote the trained and highly accomplished courtesans (almost exactly the Japanese "geisha") who entertained Greek men of means.

*Herodotus V/58
†Weigall 192

1. Though we know the names of some of Sappho's entourage, little or nothing is known about each of them or whether they were all with her at the same time. Any list should be treated with caution. The supposed names run:

Anactoria, from Miletus in Asia Minor (also the birthplace of Thales).

Gyrinno, from the island of Telos; once thought to be the same person as the poetess Erinna, said to have died at the age of nineteen. It is now virtually certain that Erinna wrote in Doric, not Aeolic, and that she lived two centuries later than Sappho.

Damoplyla, from Pamphylia on the south coast of Asia Minor. She learned to write love songs in the manner of Sappho and seems to have collected around her a group of girls.

Gongyla, from Colophon near Ephesus in Asia Minor.

Timas of Phocaea, who died young. That Sappho wrote an epitaph on Timas does not necessarily show that she was one of her circle.

Euneika, from the island of Salamis near Athens (or possibly from the town of Salamis on Cyprus).

Hero of Gyara, near the island of Andros.

Brochea, if Edmonds' surmise in line 7 of poem 27 is correct.

All the following girls apparently from Lesbos: Atthis, Praxinoa (there is a hole in the papyrus where Praxinoa's name is alleged to appear), Cydro, Telesippa, Megara, Mnasidica, Cleïs (Sappho's daughter).

For a list of the source references see Weigall 115–17. Names derived from The Suda may or may not be authentic.

Two further names have just come to light from the publication of Oxy. Pap. 2293 and 2357:

Archeanassa
Pleistodike

**3**

Edm.19. Meter, Sapphic.
Cited by Ammonius of Alexandria (writing about 400
A.D.) to show Sappho's ungrammatical use of the word
ἀρτίως as an adverb of past time "hardly had," or
"just when."

**4**

Edm.177. Meter, dactylic.
From *Etymologicum Magnum.*

**5**

Edm. Appendix 118B. Meter, as far as one can tell,
Ionic.
From a papyrus of the third century: restored conjec-
turally by Edmonds. The conjecture extends to at least
one half of this ode. The attitude, however, is typical
of Sappho.

1: What is also typical is Sappho's ability—which seems
so modern to us—to comment on an experience or
state of mind even while it is with her. Weigall writes:

> With that curious innocence of heart . . . whether it
> be actual or assumed, she compares her situation to
> that of a child whose wondering mind is intrigued
> by something new held out to it; but at the same
> time, in the one word *anoos* "unintelligent"* she
> pillories the attitude of those who forbear. . . .†

**6**

Edm.25. Meter, a choriamb and a long syllable, known
as the "Adonius" to grammarians because the three
words "O for Adonis" represent metrically the fourth
line of a Sapphic stanza. They are in fact identical with

*Here translated "imbecile."
†*Op.cit.* 216

the end of a hexameter line, though the Adonius, a colon rather than a meter, is dactylic in some contexts, choriambic in others. Here the words are probably a refrain.

7

Not given in Edm. This is a new Aeolic fragment, first published by Lobel and Page in the *Classical Quarterly* (New Series, Vol. II, XLVI) in 1952. The editors write:

> The following fragment of a papyrus-roll, written in a hand which may be assigned to the second or third century A.D., was bought by Professor O. Guéraud from the antiquary Naham on behalf of the Société Fouad de Papyrologie (P. Fouad Inv. n., 239).

The meter indicates a line of Aeolic dactyls. The authorship is ascribed to Sappho or Alcaeus. The poem is incomplete as to beginning and end, and words are missing in the fragment, which opens apparently with a reference to Apollo. I have translated according to my own reconstruction.

Lobel and Page comment:

> . . . More striking is the relation to the opening of Callimachus' Hymn to Artemis. Artemis, still a child, as she must have been in the Aeolic poem, addresses her father, Zeus, asking him to grant her perpetual virginity (ἀί πάρθενος ἔσσομαι ) and secondly to give her the mountains to live and hunt in. At the end of Artemis' prayer, Zeus nodded assent.
>
> The detail of Artemis' prayer is considerably expanded by Callimachus, but its structure and substance are the same in both.

———

Edm.138. Meter, dactylic (Aeolic pentameter, using ἦρος as "basis"): which could be represented in English by such a line:

Swallow O Swallow O why are you going

if we were to add to the beginning the words "Tell me."

Edm.31. Meter, Sapphic.
From Scholiast on Apollonius of Rhodes's *Argonautica* 3.26: "Apollonius makes Eros the son of Aphrodite, but Sappho of Earth and Heaven."
Scholiast on Theocritus 13.2: "He hesitates about whom to call Eros the son of; for Hesiod . . . and Sappho, of Aphrodite or of Earth and Heaven."
Pausanias, *Description of Greece*: "Hesiod I know has made Chaos the first creation, then Earth and Tartarus and Eros. And in the poems of Sappho of Lesbos there are many incompatible statements about Eros." Edmonds makes his hypothetical text from the quotations.

Edm.133. Meter, mainly dactylic.
From Demetrius, literary critic, *On Style:*

Charm is produced in association with ornament and through beautiful words specially shaped towards such an effect, such as . . .

Edm.93. Meter, Glyconic.
From Herodian the grammarian, *Words Unparalleled.*
The words are not explicitly attributed to Sappho.

Edm.13. Meter, dactylic pentameter.
From the *Treatise on Etymology* (tenth century A.D.).

Edm.142. Meter, dactylic pentameter, if we read παῖς and not παις.

Edm.33. Adapted from a citation of the Scholiast on Hesiod, *Works and Days* (Queenly Persuasion).

Edm.126. Meter, irregular Ionic.
From Hephaestion, *Handbook of Meter.*

1. Edmonds' ἀτίμασασ ("do you dishonor") is pure guesswork, even if scholarly guesswork. My translation "Why do you turn your back on?" could just as feasibly be "Why do you *not* turn towards." There is no certainty what word Sappho used.

Not in Edm. ἐιμ᾿ ὡς ἀπ᾿ υσσάκω λύθεισα. Meter, trochaic. From *Adesp.*46A. Not explicitly attributed to Sappho.

Edm.1. Meter, Sapphic.
Oxy.Pap.21/2288 (fragments of vv.1–21), and also from Dionysius of Halicarnassus, the celebrated rhetorician writing in Rome about 25 A.D., *Literary Composition.*

1. This is one of the very few texts of Sappho (perhaps the only text) which is both complete and undamaged.

2. Dionysius of Halicarnassus quotes the whole poem as an example of the style he calls γλαφυρὰ κὰι ἀνθηρά ("polished and colorful"). He adds:

The verbal beauty and enchantment of this passage arise from the perfect smoothness and dovetailing of every part. The words follow one another in a texture of relationships that depends on the natural grouping of the letters. . . .

3. Line 9—"swans" (line 10 in the Greek): στρôυθοι generally means "sparrows." Page is against turning them into swans and dismisses the evidence whereby the word can denote any bird, large or small:

Sappho has invoked Aphrodite to visit her on earth: and here she describes a token of proof that her prayer has been answered. Sparrows were sacred to Aphrodite, symbolic of her powers. They might be seen at any time descending suddenly to rest on earth: and it is easy to imagine that Aphrodite rode in her chariot behind them; no commoner or more satisfactory token of proof, that prayer has been answered, could be imagined or desired.*

All this is true enough, and there is also no doubt that the sparrow was notorious for wantonness and fecundity and that its flesh and eggs could be eaten as an aphrodisiac, but against it is the fact that the ostrich was known as στρουθὸς κατάγαιος ("running-along-the-ground-bird") or as στρουθοκάμηλος ("camel-bird"). In Roman times the traditional bird for drawing the car of Venus was the swan: something which the Romans could easily have borrrowed from the Greeks, as so much else. It is *not* "easy to imagine" two sparrows pulling a chariot; and is hardly less ludicrous to imagine a team of these grubby little birds in crowded formation conducting the foam-born goddess in stately flight.

4. Versions 2 and 3 given below are further attempts on the part of the translator to extract the beauty of the original.

*Denys Page 18

## Call to Aphrodite (2)

Aphrodite—deathless—chaired in splendor,
Daughter of Zeus and sweet intriguer,
Listen and do not let my heart be routed
    By sorrows, my lady.

Come as before when before you hearkened
To the faraway call of my voice and leaving
Your father's house you came on a golden
    Chariot harnessed

To the beat of the wings of your two swans teaming
Fair and strong as they hummed on high
Swift through the sky as they brought you downwards
    To the dark of the ground.

Then with a smile, O you blest lady,
Demanding on your endless features
What was it troubled me *now,* what made me
    Come to you calling

Now, and what did my wild heart want?
"Whom shall I now make over to love you?
Who is it, Sappho, that's offending?
    Let her be running,

Soon she'll run after. Let her refuse your
Gifts, she'll be giving. Let her not love you,
Soon she'll be loving—like it or no—" . . .
    O come to me now,

Unloose me again from this merciless craving:
Do what I long to have done—O my own
    Comrade in battle.


## Call to Aphrodite (3)

Undying and dapple-throned Aphrodite,
Daughter of Zeus and weaver of ruses,
Keep, I beg you, my lady, from breaking
    My spirit in anguish.

---

Come to me now as before when you heard me
Cry to you far away—cry and you heeded:
Came to me leaving the house of your father;
    Harnessed the golden

Chariot—swan-drawn, beautiful strong-winged
Pinions beating the mid air of heaven
Down to the dark of the earth and arriving
    Suddenly there. Oh,

Blessed the smile on your undying features,
Asking what ailed me now and what made me
Call on you now and what did my raving
    Heart beseech help for?

"Whom shall I now make over to love you?
Sappho, who hurts you? Ah, if she flees you
Soon she'll be chasing. If she won't take your
    Gifts, she'll be giving.

If she won't love you, soon she'll be loving,
Like it or no." . . . Oh, now come again:
Loosen me free from this raving pain.
Make that to happen what happen I want so,
    With *you* as my ally.

### 18

Edm.5. Meter, Sapphic.
From Strabo, *Geography* and Athenaeus, *Doctors at Dinner*. Linked by Athenaeus to the last stanza of poem 45, though on the potsherd text of this poem recently discovered these words are not included.

1. The fragment is, of course, addressed to Aphrodite. It was a regular feature of prayers and hymns to mention all the likely addresses. Milton in *Lycidas* "Where were ye nymphs . . ." is imitating Theocritus doing the same sort of thing, though it is switched from a prayer to a reproach.

2. Aphrodite, the Foam-born, rose out of the sea and first put foot to land on the island of Cyprus (though the island of Cythera and even others claim that dis-

tinction). There were several centers of her worship in Cyprus: Paphos was one of them.

3. The Panormus intended is probably either the town in Sicily (Palermo) or the capital of the island of Samos, about a hundred and fifty miles from Lesbos.

## 19

Edm.23. Meter, Sapphic.
From the *Treatise on Etymology*.

## 20

Edm.17.
From the *Old Treatise on Etymology (Vet. Etymologicum Magnum)*:

> μελεδῶναι *"cares": the worries that eat away the mind . . . and the Aeolic writers talk of pain as* σταλαγμός *"a dripping"; compare Sappho . . .*

## 21

Edm.27. Apollonius on *Pronouns:*

> ῎Αμμε: "us" or "me" in Aeolic.

Sappho possibly means Eros or Aphrodite.

## 22

Edm.20. Meter, Sapphic.
From the Scholiast (commentator) on Aristophanes' *Peace*.

1. Haines and others read the MS ἐκάλυπτε for ἐπέτεννε. In which case one would translate μάσλης as: a leather thong or sandals, and the fragment could mean:

> Her feet were hidden in a pair of gaily decorated sandals, a beautiful piece of Lydian workmanship.

---

Hill translates:

> She wore an embroidered leather girdle, the ends
> of which reached down to her feet, etc.

2: The words occur very likely in an invocation to
Aphrodite.

### 23

Edm.54. Meter, Sapphic-14-syllables.
From Maximus of Tyre, essayist (c.150 A.D.), *Dissertations:*

> Socrates is frantic with love of Phaedrus, and
> Sappho's heart is set trembling with love (by Love)
> like a squall that hits the oak trees.

1. Some editors read κὰτ'ὄρος instead of κατάρης
which gives us: a squall falling "from the mountains."

2. It is possible that Sappho has in mind Anactoria,
whom Maximus of Tyre equates with Phaedrus.

### 24

Given in Edm. Vol. III, as Adespota 40. Meter, Aeolic:
(what used to be called "logaoedic").
From *Adesp.*77, but not explicitly attributed to Sappho
and usually considered doubtful.

### 25

Not in Edm: πόθεν δέ τὠλκος εὖπεζες ἔβλης: Meter,
Sapphic.
From *Adesp.*75. Not explicitly ascribed to Sappho.

### 26

Edm.42. Meter, Sapphic.
From a second-century papyrus. Only four words in
the Greek, included somewhat unconvincingly by Ed-

monds in the last stanza of his No. 42 (my poem No. 152).

**27**

Edm.2. Meter, Sapphic.
Quoted by "Longinus," the Greek philosopher and essayist, writing about 250 A.D., *On the Sublime.*\* The poem is incomplete but with *Call to Aphrodite* (17) is one of the most famous of all Sappho's love songs. Catullus—middle of the first century B.C.—in the course of his tortured affair with "Lesbia" wrote a version of it which became celebrated. Plutarch, writing about 70 A.D., also mentions it.

1. It is not certain to whom the poem is addressed, though it is often called *The Ode to Anactoria.* Perhaps it refers to Atthis. From poem 53 it seems that Anactoria had been the favorite of Atthis rather than of Sappho.

2. Longinus in his treatise says:

> Sappho . . . in every case renders the symptoms of love-madness by its actual and visible concomitants. But where exactly does she show her genius? Precisely in the skill with which she first chooses then combines the best and most typical of those symptoms.

After quoting the poem by way of illustration, he goes on:

> Is it not astonishing how Sappho beats and drives into it soul and body, hearing, speech, sight, and flesh—all as distinct elements—yet by opposites is both frozen and scorched, raves and is sane, and actually fears she is nearly dead, so that she expresses not one passion but a congress of passions?

---

\*It is now generally agreed that this Longinus cannot have written the work in question, which quotes nothing later than the age of Augustus.

─────────

3. Line 7: I have adopted Page as against Edmonds. In Edm. the line runs:

ὡς γὰρ ἔς τ᾽ἴδω, Βρόχε᾽, ως με φώῶς
(My voice when I see you, O Brochea!)

4. All that is left of the fifth stanza is the first line:

ἀλλὰ πα`ν τολμάτν ἐπὲι πρνητα
(But I must bear with it all because now I'm a beggar . . .)

### 28

Edm.52. Meter, Sapphic-14-syllables.
From Chrisippus, grammarian and Stoic philosopher c.220 B.C., *On Negatives.*

### 29

Edm.53. Meter, Sapphic-14-syllables.
From Herodian the grammarian, *Words Without Parallel.*

### 30

Edm.56 and 57. Meter, Sapphic-14-syllables.
From Herodian the grammarian, *Words Without Parallel:* on the use of the word τύλη "cushion."

### 31

Edm.29. Meter, Sapphic.
From Julian the Apostate (last pagan Roman emperor) in *Letter to Eugenius:*

Yes, I should even fly to the foot of your mountain so that I could, in Sappho's words, my beloved, embrace you.

## 32

Edm.3. Meter, Sapphic.
From Eustathius, literary critic, on the *Iliad*. Confirmed by Julian, *Letters* 19.

*33*

Edm.72. Meter, choriambic (greater Asclepiad).
From Chrysippus, grammarian, *Negatives*.

1. It is not known to which of her young companions Sappho refers.

*34*

Edm.124. Meter, perhaps choriambic.
Apollonius on *Pronouns*.

*35*

Edm.22. Meter, Sapphic.
Apollonius on *Pronouns*: as used by the Aeolic writers.

*36*

Edm.132. *Treatise on Words (Etymologicum Magnum)*.

*37*

Edm.68. Meter, choriambic (greater Asclepiad), i.e., Sapphic-16-syllables.
From the *Argument to Theocritus*, No. 28.

1. Usually put among Sappho's Epithalamia. Possibly but not certainly the opening of a bridal song.

*38*

Edm.Appendix 86A. Meter, Sapphic with a form of Glyconic.
A comparatively new fragment, first restored by Ed-

monds in the Cambridge Philological Society's *Proceedings*, 1927. Given in Lobel *Sapphous Mele* p. 80.

1. Weigall comments:

> Sappho . . . supplies a sad little picture of herself vainly trying to write what was obviously a commissioned hymn to Adonis, but being distracted by her own thoughts.*

### 39

Not given in Edm. although it is certainly part of his fragment 86 and my No. 53. They are given clearly in Lobel and Page as lines 21 and 22.

### 40

Edm.118A, Appendix. Meter, Sapphic-16-syllables.
Almost nothing remains of the original. I have translated Edmonds's reconstruction freely, making sense (perhaps) of a baffling non sequitur.

### 41

Edm.129. Meter, trochaic.
From Hephaestion, *Handbook of Meter.*

### 42

Edm.40. Meter, Sapphic.
Second- and third-century papyruses: Oxy.Pap.1231 fragment I, col.ii/2–21 + 2166 (a)/3; and 2289 fragment 9.

1. Lines 11 to 20 reconstructed by Wiliamowitz, Vitelli, Edmonds, and others: largely conjectural.

2. Sappho is asking for a same passage back to Mytilene after a tour abroad. Weigall thinks she may be returning from a visit to the island of Samos, a journey by

*Weigall 183

sea of about a hundred and fifty miles from Lesbos. Since Samos was a recognized center of Greek culture and the chief seat of the worship of the goddess Hera, it is inconceivable that Sappho did not at some time visit it. Edmonds entertains the possibility that she is here preparing to embark at Syracuse for Mytilene after hearing of the amnesty from her (second) exile.

3. Thyone was the deified Semele, whom Zeus impregnated during a visitation of thunder and lightning, thus engendering the god Dionysus.

### 43

Edm.41. Meter, Sapphic.
From a second-century papyrus: Oxy.Pap.1931/9. Very little of the text is certain: reconstructed conjecturally by Edmonds.

1. Again we do not know if Sappho had a specific voyage in mind.

2. Merchant vessels were large. Sail power was supplemented by oars; speed must have been about five knots. See Weigall 239, Apollonius of Rhodes i/601 ff., Herodotus iv/86, Thucydides ii/97 and many other citations.

### 44

Edm.87. Meter, Aeolic.
From Athenaeus, *Doctors at Dinner*, commenting on a piece about handkerchiefs he had come across in a book called *The Guide to Asia*. He related the information to Sappho's lines.

1. The poem recounts (probably) a dream: Timas has sent the handkerchief for the statue of Aphrodite in Sappho's house in Lesbos. This perhaps is Sappho's letter of thanks.

2. Timas, who died young (see poem 163), was an Ionian from Phocaea, a city on the mainland of Asia

Minor south of Mytilene. It was the northernmost member of the important Ionian Confederacy.

3. πορφύρα: "purple," or shades of dark red: strictly the "purple-fish," the Purpura and the Murex, species of shellfish. Tyre on the coast of Syria became the center of the purple trade. Because of its costliness purple became the color of kings.

## 45

Only fragments given by Edm. in 4 and 6. Meter, Sapphic.
This poem, written on a potsherd in a hand assigned to the third century B.C., is one of the oldest records we have of the text of Sappho. The poem is not complete: the beginning and probably the end are missing. Hermogenes, *Kings of Style*, writing about 170 A.D., quotes the second stanza (Edm.4). This is the description that has often been identified with the Garden of the Nymphs which Demetrius (writing on style about 150 A.D.) says Sappho sang of. Athenaeus, *Doctors at Dinner*, quotes all but the beginning of the fourth stanza (writing about 230 A.D.)

1. Cox (79), commenting on the second stanza (which was then thought to be a fragment on its own), says:

> The sound of the words, the repetition of the long vowels, particularly ω, the poetic imagery of the whole and the drowsy cadence of the last two words gives this fragment a combination of qualities probably not surpassed in any language.*

2. Line 10 (in the Greek and English): prior to Page most editors accepted ἀι δ'ἄνητοι ("and the dill") instead of ἀι δ'ἄηται ("and the rushes of wind"). Taking the former reading and keeping πνέοισιν ("they blow"), I should then change my rendering to:

*Cos 79

Here is a meadow, horses feeding,
Spring profuse with flowers, and scented
   Dill with breezes.

3. Fourth stanza: Athenaeus does not give the first line as it appears to be written on the shard. He has simply: ἔλθε Κύπρι ("come, Cypris"). On the shard there appears to be ἔνθα δή σὺ ("there indeed you"), then a word of two syllables is missing, then comes ἔλοισα Κύπρι ("bring, Cypris") finishing the line. The missing word looks as though it may have been στεμματ' and although Page doubts the τ and ε this is what I have translated.

4. The first mention of frankincense in extant Greek literature. Homer nowhere speaks of the burning of incense. It was probably introduced from Egypt (where it was in regular use long before the Mycenean era) little if at all earlier than the seventh century B.C. See Denys Page, 36.

### 46

Edm.123. Hephaestion, *Handbook of Meter*, exemplifying Ionic trimeter.

### 47

Edm.9. Meter, Sapphic.
Apollonius, *Syntax*.

1. Hill translates: "May I win the toss this time."

### 48

Edm.7. Meter, Sapphic.
Apollonius, *Pronouns*.

1. White she-goats were sacrificed to Aphrodite Pandemos (All the People's).

Edm.89. Meter, choriambic.
Adapted from Julian, *Letter to Iamblichus*.

Edm.96. Meter, choriambic.
Herodian, grammarian, *Words Without Parallel*.

1. Haines thinks the fragment is possibly from Alcaeus.
There are numerous readings.

Edm.44. Meter, Sapphic.
From a second-century papyrus: Oxy.Pap.1231/14.
Heavily reconstructed by Edmonds.

1. The name of the girl is unknown. Helen, mother of
Hermione, is one move more divine.

Edm.46. Meter, Sapphic.
From a second-century papyrus. Heavily reconstructed
by Hunt, Lobel, and Edmonds.

1. It is not known to whom Sappho is speaking.

2. In line 5. Page's στείχομεν γὰρ ἐς γάμον is right
and supersedes Edmonds's guess of πλάσιον.

Edm.86. Meter, a mixture of hendecasyllable with
Glyconic.
From a sixth-century parchment. Much of the first
stanza is lost and the name "Atthis" is conjectural.
Page assumes the poem to have been longer by five or
six stanzas, of which he gives only scattered words.
See notes to Nos. 38 and 39. Page seems to give the
total number of lines in this poem as thirty-six. My

text is compiled mainly from Edmonds and Page, except for the last stanza which I adopt from Hill.

1. This is a song to comfort Atthis (see poem 109) who has lost a favorite companion.

2. Sardis: capital of Lydia in Asia Minor. A place of culture and sophistication.

3. Line 9 of the Greek (7 and 8 in the English): I make a new suggestion for the perplexing βροδοδάκτυλος ("rosy-fingered"): even at sunset the moon can hardly be described as that. If two letters are changed, β and δ, we get δροσοδάκτυλος ("dewy-finger"). Diffidently I suggest that this is what Sappho wrote and I print it in my text.

### 54

Edm.83. Meter, mainly Glyconic: the third line of each stanza has an extra dactyl.
From a sixth-century parchment.

1. The poem may be a record of Sappho's painful separation from Atthis, her favorite (see note on poem 109). Bowra's comment is: "words of sheer and absolute sorrow."* Page with his customary astringency says:

> It may be that Sappho was distressed, and truly sought consolation in tender memories; or it may be that she was more concerned to entertain her audience with a description of delights which they at least have not yet forgone. The sorrowful leave-taking may be no more than a conventional occasion for that description. The summary narrative of the parting, the self-control of Sappho, and the great length and placid spirit of the tale of their pleasures, are all easily reconciled with such a conception of the purpose of the poem as a whole.†

*Bowra 197
†Denys Page 83

2. Professor A. W. Gomme writes: "Surely Schubart was right in suggesting, as he once did, that the first line was spoken by the girl who was leaving. . . . It is not Sappho speaking of her *present* despair by contrast with the comforting words she used to her companion (vv.6–20, the rest of the poem), as Page understands it. It is she, not Sappho, who is weeping and in despair. . . . This is clearer if, as Page suggests we should do, we mark a pause at the end of v.2, so that v.3 will mean "this too she often said to me." (*Journal of Hellenic Studies*, LXXVV [Part II] 1957.)

3. 8th stanza: tantalizingly incomplete. Page allows only:

Καὶ στρώμν[αν ἐ]πὶ μολθάκαν
ἀπάλαν πα. [      ] . . . ων
ἐξίησ πόθο[ν ]. νίδων
("And on soft beds . . . you would satisfy your longing. . . .")

He adds characteristically:

There are obvious indications that it contained matter incompatible with the modern theory of Sappho's character.* No useful purpose would be served by reporting the desperate shifts by which some modern scholars have attempted to eliminate these indications.†

But Edmonds writes:

. . . the reference is doubtless to eating and drinking; we are not justified, *in this context*, in putting any other interpretation upon the passage.‡

I have adhered to Edmonds rather than Page.

*Page implies that by this theory Sappho is whitewashed from all taint of Lesbianism. For his own theory, far less favorable to Sappho, see his *Sappho and Alcaeus*, pp. 142–46.
†Denys Page 83
‡Edmonds 433

4. Edmonds has this note:

> Greek men (after Homer) reclined at meals; *at Athens* it was usual for the women of the household to dine apart and to sit; but the hetairai when sharing the men's symposia reclined like them.*

It should be noted, however, that this is almost certainly not true of Sappho's Lesbos, where women had equal status with men (or almost).

## 55

Edm.38. Meter, Sapphic.
From a second-century papyrus: Oxy.Pap.1231 fragment i + 2166(a)2.

1. This poem was first made known to the world by the Egypt Exploration Society in 1914. My text is principally from Page, except for lines 12 to 14 and the whole of the sixth stanza (which is from Edmonds and largely conjectural). The poem is almost complete.

2. It is apparent that Anactoria had married and left Sappho's circle to go and live in Lydia. See poem 53.

3. The meaning of the second stanza depends on whether we read with Edmonds περσκέθοισα "surpassed," or with Page περσκόπεισα "had examined," "was acquainted with." I have taken the first. The sense of the second would be that Helen, though she had wide experience of male excellence, chose the deplorable Paris—because she loved him—a testimony to the blinding power of love. Unfortunately, the rest of the text in either reading does not support such clear sense. I have taken περσκέθοισα from Edmonds, but the rest of the verse from Page.

*Ibid. 433

183

## 56

Edm.107. Meter, choriambic.
From Athenaeus, *Doctors at Dinner,* Clearchus speaking:

It is quite natural that those who see themselves as
beautiful and blooming should gather flowers. . . .

After which he uses Sappho's words indirectly.

*57*

Edm.139. Meter, dactylic hexameter.
From Athenaeus, *Doctors at Dinner.*

1. I have translated Sappho's 'ερεβινθεος as *genista*
(broom). The Lexicons give it as chick-pea, but I
know of no member of the vetch or pulse family with
yellow flowers. She could have meant gorse (furz),
whose flowers are indeed golden, but gorse does not
ordinarily grow along the seashore. In all cases the
plant would belong to the family of Leguminosa (peas
and beans).

*58*

Edm.67. Meter, 14-syllable.
From the Scholiast on Aristophanes:

Young people and lovers used to weave garlands.
This refers to the custom among the ancients whereby
the women wove garlands; cf. Sappho.

1. Edmonds thinks this line may belong to the Ode to
Hector and Andromache, poem 82.

*59*

Edm.30. Meter, Sapphic.
Reconstituted from a citation by Philostratus, *Pictures,*
and from Aristaenetus, *Letters.* The former:

And in this way the girls vied with one another;
rosy-armed, pert-eyed, lovely-cheeked, honey-voiced
—this (last) is Sappho's exquisite image.

## 60

Edm.64. Meter, Glyconic.
From Pollux, *Vocabulary:* "Anacreon . . . says that
dill (anise) too was used for garlands, as indeed by
Sappho and Alcaeus. The two latter also speak of
parsley."

The word used is Σελινον (Selinon). It is not certain which
of the enormous family of the Umbelliferae is meant.
The leaves of the water parsley—"apium graveolens,"
allied to our celery—were often used for chaplets on
account of their strong fragrance. Crowns of wild
parsley—"that long remains green," in Virgil's later
description—were given as prizes in the Isthmian and
Nemean games. By the time of Pindar (not long after
Sappho), this seems to have been a wreath of dry
"Selinon."

## 61

Edm.94. Meter, Aeolic.
From Demetrius on *Style:*

> One might adduce many similar instances of charm.
> There can be charm, too, in the form of a trope or
> metaphor, as of the cricket . . .

Demetrius does not specifically assign this description
to Sappho.

## 62

Edm.130. Meter, trochaic.
Hephaestion, *Handbook of Meter.*

1. Cleïs appears to have been Sappho's only child,
named after Sappho's mother. Weigall thinks she may
have been born during the exile in Sicily, on the ground

---

that the Cleïs in poem 150 (if indeed the text is correct) was obviously old enough to help about the house when Sappho was still young. She is mentioned altogether three times in Sappho's extant fragments. See also poem 133.

## 63

Edm.95. Meter, choriambic.
From Zenobius (c.130 A.D.), *Centuries of Proverbs:*

> [The expression is] used of those who die young, or of people who love children but spoil them. For Gello was a girl who died before her time, and the inhabitants of Lesbos say her ghost haunts little children; and they put down to her the death of those that die early. It comes in Sappho.

Gello causes the death of little children by her famished kisses.

## 64

Edm.115. Meter, Ionic a majore: treated by modern metricists as a form of choriambic.
From Hephaestion, *Handbook of Meter.*

1. Mnasidika must be the same girl as the Dika of the next fragment (65). Nothing has come to light about her.

2. Gyrinno or Gyrinna is mentioned by Maximus of Tyre, the essayist, who draws a parallel between Sappho's circle and Socrates' and sets Gyrinno first as corresponding to Alcibiades, Socrates's favorite. Weigall thinks she is to be identified with the poetess Erinna, who came from the island of Telos off Rhodes near the southwestern coast of Asia Minor. Erinna composed an epic poem of three hundred lines, called *The Distaff,* which was famous in antiquity. Only a few lines remain. She died at the age of nineteen. It is now generally acknowledged that she wrote in Doric, not Aeolic, about two hundred years *after* Sappho.

---

**65**

Edm.117. Meter, Sapphic-16-syllables.
Oxy.Pap.XV/1787/33, and from Athenaeus, *Doctors at Dinner* (on garlands):

> Aeschylus . . . says plainly that the reason we put wreaths on our heads is to honor Prometheus and make up for his chains. . . . But Sappho gives a simpler reason than atonement for our self-crowning and says . . .

**66**

Not in Edm. but D 68 and LP 65. From a third-century papyrus: Oxy.Pap.1787.6. Meter, Ionic tetrameter of 16 syllables.
More than half of the extant lines are missing. I have been jejune but made my own reconstruction. Barnstone suggests that Mika is a shortened form of Mnasidika. Penthilos (though himself long dead) was still an important political name in Lesbos.

**67**

Edm.97. Meter, perhaps choriambic.
From the *Treatise on Etymology*.

1. According to one tradition, Leda brought forth *two* eggs after her affair with Zeus-turned-swan. One hatched Helen and Clytemnestra, and the other the twins Castor and Pollux.

2. Though we translate the word ὑάκινθος by "hyacinth," it is by no means certain what flower was meant. Cox says:

> The Greek word ὑάκινθος does not mean the flower which at the present day is called "hyacinth." The Greek name was applied to several flowers, of which one was almost certainly the larkspur, and another,

as noted elsewhere (in the fragment, for instance) the Iris.*

3. If one reads ὑακίνθινον instead of ὑακίνθωι as I have done, one might translate it: ". . . an egg of hyacinth blue."

## 68

Edm.101. Meter, choriambic of 15 syllables without basis, (sometimes called "the greater Sapphic").
Hephaestion, *Handbook of Meter*. Also quoted by Attilius Fortunatus and by Servius as an example of the choriambic tetrameter.

## 69

Edm.73. Meter, choriambic (greater Asclepiad).
From Aldus, grammarian, in *Cornucopia*.

1. Gyara is a barren island off Ceos and Andros.

## 70

Edm.59,60,61,62: fragments which probably belong to separate poems, epigrams or riddles. I have put them all together. Meter, 14-syllable.
From Demetrius on *Style*, Athenaeus *Doctors at Dinner*, Gregorius on Hermogenes.
Demetrius:

The appeal of comedy, particularly, depends on hyperbole; and every hyperbole is an impossibility. For instance, this is Aristophanes . . . And so are such phrases as "healthier than a cucumber," "balder than a calm sea" and Sappho's . . .

Gregorius:

*Cox 113

The ear is improperly tickled by such erotic tricks
of phrase as are found in Anacreon and Sappho, as
for instance . . .*

### 71

Edm.75. Meter, choriambic (lesser Asclepiad) with a
line of twelve syllables.
From Maximus of Tyre, essayist, in *Dissertations*.

### 72

Edm. 167. Meter, possibly Sapphic-16-syllables.
From the Scholiast on Apollonius of Rhodes in the
latter's poem *Argonautica* (c.200 B.C.). It is not clear
whether the words are Sappho's or Apollonius's. The
Scholiast writes:

The love story of Selene (the Moon) is told by
Sappho . . . and there it is said that Selene comes
down to Endymion in this cave.

1. Weigall thinks that Sappho is the originator of the
famous legend in which the Moon-goddess sees and
falls in love with the young shepherd Endymion asleep
in his cave on Mount Latmos: keeping him there eter-
nally young and enjoying the passions she rouses him
to in his dreams.

She understood the reason why the goddess came
night after night to the beautiful shepherd, yet would
not permit him to awake. The Moon-goddess in her
poem was herself: Endymion was ideal youth, phys-
ically to be desired, and in slumber not to be
feared, a man in the response of breath to breath,
of caress to caress, but not a man in that forcefulness
which displeased her. Something in her tempera-
ment, moreover, reached with warmth to the thought

---

*With such innocuousness condemned, no wonder future puritanism
was to heap Sappho's nine books onto the bonfire!

of Selene's active, not passive, part in these tender
pleasures of the night.*

**73**

ἐγω φαῖμι Ϝιοπλόκωι
Μοῖσαν ευ λάλεμεν

Edm. Vol. III, Adespota 25.
Meter, doubtful; or choriambic with first two words
used as basis.
From Plut., Garr. 5 (Bergk, Adesp., p. 53). Haines
thinks this fragment possibly by Alcaeus.

**74**

Edm.10. Meter, Sapphic.
From Appolonius on *Pronouns*.

**75**

Edm.32. Meter, Sapphic.
From Himerius, *Declamations*.

**76**

Edm.149. Meter, dactylic hexameter: found chiefly in
Sappho's epithalamia, from which this fragment is taken.
Quoted by Demetrius (literary critic c.150 A.D.), *On
Style:*

> Sometimes, too, Sappho achieves her charm through
> repetition, as in this passage on the Evening Star . . .

**77**

Edm.80. Meter, Glyconic.
Hermogenes, *On Kinds of Oratory*, talking of sweet-
ness or charm:

*Weigall 283

... and when Sappho takes to her lyre and it answers her.

Eustathius, *Iliad* xi/41, also mentions the fact that Sappho spoke to her lyre.

1. The word Sappho uses meant originally a tortoise-shell. Here it means a lyre.

2. Hermes is credited in mythology with having invented the first lyre by stretching strings across the cavity of the tortoiseshell. This became its sound box, the curved horns of a goat its arms.

3. As a musician Sappho seems to have been something of an innovator. A new form of harp with twenty strings is attributed to her by Athenaeus, and also the plectrum for striking the strings with. According to Aristoxenus she invented the mixolydian mode. There have been many guesses by scholars and musicologists as to what exactly this was. Aristoxenus describes it as: "particularly sensuous and emotive."

### 78

Edm.16. Meter, Sapphic.
From the Scholiast on Pindar:

> He gives us a vivid picture of the eagle perched on Zeus's scepter and, lulled to sleep by the music, relaxing both its wings. . . . Sappho on the other hand talks of the doves . . .

The MS. reading is ψυχρός (chill), emended for better sense to ψαυχρος (swift or light), which in the context I translate as "faint-headed."

### 79

Not in Edm. meter doubtful. From an Oxyrhynchus of the second century A.D. See Campbell No. 214, frag. 4. The phrase "first trickle" filling the gap in the papyrus is my own conjecture.

## 80

Edm.45. Meter, Sapphic.
From a second-century papyrus: Oxy.Pap.1231/15.
The first and last stanzas are reconstructed by Hunt,
Lobel, and Edmonds.

1. Basing myself on a text printed by Hill and making
my own reconstruction, I give the following as a plau-
sible reading:

> Oh, come back to me, I ask you, as quickly as you
> can—my rosebud, Gongyla, carrying your milk-white
> sail. My own longing surely is the breeze that blows
> you along, you exquisite thing. Yes, my tremulous
> heart is ready to see you come into port . . . and
> I—happy.

## 81

Edm.24. Meter, Sapphic.
From Philodemus, *Piety* (c.60 B.C.; discovered at
Herculaneum).

1. There is some doubt whether Hecate or Peitho
(goddess of persuasion) is being addressed. The latter—
called daughter of Aphrodite—was, together with Hera,
Artemis, Urania, and Aphrodite herself, one of the
goddesses to whom sacrifice was made before the wed-
ding ceremony.

Edm.66. Meter, a Sapphic variation of the epic dacty-
lic hexameter: almost dactylic pentameter with an in-
variable fourteen syllables. Haines classes it among
the choriambic or Aeolic rhythms characteristic of the
Sapphic stanza (i.e., basically the trochee mingled with
the dactyl).
From a third-century papyrus: Oxy.Pap.1232 fragment
I.coll.ii/iii, and 2076 col.ii.

1. Page and others think it possible (but unprovable until we have more evidence) that this ode was a wedding song sung at a real wedding. To Sappho's hearers it would have had a slightly archaic ring, suggesting a saga that went back hundreds of years to the heroic age. In point of fact, this poem—a comparatively recent discovery in the sands of Egypt—proves what had long been suspected, that Sappho, although usually composing in her own vernacular (Lesbian Aeolic), did occasionally borrow from epic dialect, vocabulary, and style. This ode, though for the most part Lesbian, imitates in several places Homeric phraseology. Sappho calls on two traditions, blending old and new. Meanwhile the pictures she draws (as Page points out) is not taken from any epic model but from contemporary life.

3. Thebe is in Mysia, not to be confused with Thebes in Boeotia.

4. The words myrrh, cassia, frankincense, do not (according to Page) appear in any extant Greek literature before the time of Sappho, nor does Homer anywhere mention the burning of incense. See note on poem 45.

### 83

Edm.146. Meter, Aeolic.
From Athenaeus, *Doctors at Dinner*.

1. Haines suggests the marriage of Peleus and Thetis, or possibly Heracles and Hebe, is being alluded to in this wedding song.

2. It could have been sung by the bridegroom's party as a stirrup cup before the bridegroom set out for the bride's house, though more likely as the toast at the actual wedding banquet itself.

3. The bridegroom, having been bathed in sacred water—his hair curled, scented, and crowned with a wreath of flowers—sets off toward sunset for the house of the bride and her parents. He and the best man are

mounted on a chariot drawn by two horses or·mules. A noisy crowd of young men accompany them. Music greets them at the bride's house, which, like the bridegroom's, is festooned with laurel, ivy, bay, and olive. He enters the canopy of greenery to the dinner party which precedes the marriage ceremony. It was in the course of the dinner that the above toast was probably sung (and it must be remembered that this is only a fragment).*

4. At ordinary banquets the preliminary drink from which the libation was poured was unmixed wine, but the real drinking did not begin till the main courses had been served and eaten. The wine was poured into the water—not vice versa—and honey and spices sometimes added. Then a little was spilt onto the ground as a further libation and a hymn or song sung. Naked boys poured the wine for the guests—who, at Athens at least, did not include women unless hetairai. Athenaeus *Doctors at Dinner* writes:

> It was the custom among the ancients for the boys of noblest birth to pour out the wine. . . . The beautiful Sappho sings the praises of her brother Larichus as serving the wine in the town hall of Mytilene.

It is possible that women dined with men in Sappho's Lesbos, though this was not later Greek practice even apart from Athens. We know now from recent Etruscan discoveries in Italy that the Etruscan men and women dined together, sitting on couches. Though the Etruscan link with the Lydians (neighbors to Lesbos) is still only an hypothesis, it is tempting to make it throw light on what we know of the Lesbians (as well as on the Ionians and Trojans). See note 4 to poem 54.

*See Weigall 202ff.

194

## 84

Edm.191. Meter, dactylic.
From Pollux, *Vocabulary*:

> Mid-bossed cups and bath-stopper cups get their
> names from their shape, but the gold-bossed from
> the substance of which they are made, like Sappho's
> gold cup with a twisted node.

*85*

Edm.161. Meter, dactylic.
From Hephaestion, *Handbook of Meter*.
See note 3 to poem 83.

1. The bridegroom would normally be several years
older than the bride and at least twenty. Probably he
would have kept a mistress* for some years previously,
"continence being regarded" (in Weigall's phrase), "as
unwholesome." The favorite time for weddings was
the month of Gamelion (γάμος wedding), which came
between the end of January and the beginning of
February, it being thought a good thing if the first
child could be born at the beginning of the winter. In
February the Greek spring is not far off.

*86*

Edm.148. Meter, dactylic hexameter with refrain.
From Demetrius, *On Style* (c.150 A.D.)

1. This bridal ditty might have been sung as the groom
entered the bride's house, but more probably when he

---

*My friend Donald Lucas (Cambridge University) in a letter com-
ments: "We know nothing of Lesbian society at this time except
what can be gleaned from Sappho and Alcaeus, and this tells us
little about keeping a mistress. In a slave-owning society sexual
experience is not hard to come by, but I much doubt if a youth still
living at home would 'keep' a mistress. Weigall's information is
compiled from many times and places."

came back to his own after the bridal dinner, bringing the bride with him. They returned sitting together on the driving seat of his chariot, with the best man behind. A procession of men and women carrying torches and a group of singing bridesmaids, led by a flute player, accompanied the pair who "set out under a shower of flowers and a battery of cheers, jeers, and good wishes. The bridegroom's mother met them at the door of his home; and as the bride crossed the threshold, the pair were pelted with confetti and grain, while the company sang the hymenaean hymn as above, which corresponded to the modern wedding march."*

2. "The singer of Lesbos": Cox thinks it possible that Terpander is meant, but the line may be merely a reference to Lesbian poets in general. Terpander, the lyric poet, was at the height of his genius about thirty years before Sappho was born. It is also perfectly possible that Sappho means herself.

**87**

Edm.105. Meter, choriambic.
From Pollux, *Vocabulary*.

1. Hill takes the text as:

Ἀμφὶ δ'ἄβροις λαδίοις ἐν τετύκασσεν

and translates:

> She wrapped herself up well in a soft woolen garment.

2. Weigall, gleaning his basic information from the *Dictionary of Antiquities*, writes:

> Weddings always took place in the evening. Some time during the afternoon the bride was given a

*Weigall 203

ceremonial bath in holy-water obtained from some
sacred well or stream, after which she was dressed
in fine new clothes and a veil of transparent cambric
was draped about her and over her flower-wreathed
head, but not so as to conceal her rouged and
painted little face or her hands with their well-
manicured and red-stained fingernails.*

## 88

Edm.157. Meter. Glyconic.
Reconstructed by Edmonds from Himerius, the rheto-
rician, *Wedding Song of Severus.*

1. The bride could be as young as fourteen among the
Ionians, but not less than seventeen or eighteen among
the Lesbians.

## 89

Edm.158. Meter, Aeolic.
From Choricius, *Wedding Song of Zachary:*

> And so to please you again I shall ornament your
> bride with a song of Sappho's.

## 90

Edm.163. Meter, choriambic.
From Dionysius of Halicarnassus, *On Literary Com-
position.*

1. According to Aristaenetus, a writer of imaginary
letters who flourished about 450 A.D., Sappho ob-
served a stock order in her compositions for nuptials:
she opened with an invocation to the Muses and Graces,
and followed up with praises of the bride and groom.
Himerius, the rhetorician (who wrote a hundred and
fifty years earlier), says:

*Weigall 202–03

It was her custom to liken the bridegroom to Achilles, comparing the young man's exploits to this hero's.

## 91

Edm.153. Meter, dactylic.
From *Inedita* (MS. in Paris) edited by Cramer, Oxford. 1.71.19.

## 92

Edm.150 and 151. Meter, hexameter.
From Scholiast on Hermogenes, *Kinds of Style*, and Demetrius, *On Style*.

1. In his detailed description of a wedding, Weigall says:

> The actual wedding ceremony was simple: the bridegegroom took the bride's hand and led her to the altar of the household gods, a boy playing a flute walking ahead, and women holding flaming torches flanking them. No vows were made, but this presentation of the bride to the domestic gods of the bridegroom's family legalized the union; and immediately afterwards the bride's new mother-in-law led her to the bedroom, the bridemaids pushing the girl from behind.*

2. Cox thinks that:

> The "sweet apple" to which Sappho refers was probably the result of a graft of apple on quince.†

Against this: the quince is yellow, not red; besides, it is only pears that are grafted onto quince. I asked the Royal Horticultural Society if Sappho could possibly have meant the sugar apple (*Annona squamosa*) or

*Weigall 203–04
†Cox, Edwin Marion, *The Poems of Sappho.*

perhaps the persimmon, which is orange-red and known in Italy as "dolce mele," "sweet apple"—exactly translating Sappho's γλυκύμαλον. I print the Royal Horticultural Society's detailed reply to my query:

In reply to your inquiry concerning the "Sugar Apple," *Annona squamosa*, this is a small deciduous tree some 15–20 ft. in height, from tropical America. It has been widely cultivated in tropical areas for its greenish-yellow, glaucous fruits and has been known prior to the nineteenth century in Asia, where in some places it appears naturalized. I do not think however this could be the plant to which Sappho was referring as there is no evidence of earlier introduction into the East.

With regard to the Persimmon, *Diospyros kaki*, this is native to China and Japan and was first known in British gardens about 1790. A related species, *D. lotus*, known as the "Date Plum" was introduced towards the end of the sixteenth century and is native to Western Asia and the Himalaya.

There is, however, as far as I can trace, no evidence that either of these species was cultivated in ancient Greece. I think probably that Sappho was in fact referring to an Apple, perhaps not in the sense we know it today, but certainly a cultivated variety. The Apple has largely been derived from *Malus pumila*, a very variable species found wild in Western Asia, the Caucasus and Southern Europe and according to all the records has been cultivated from time immemorial. It was certainly grown by the ancient Etruscans and Pliny and other writers mention it many times. Epicurus (270 B.C.) certainly cultivated Apples and used methods, such as root pruning, which are still in use today. The famous botanist, De Candolle, in his book *The Origin of Cultivated Plants*, states: "The country in which the Apple appears to be most indigenous is the region between Trebizond (on the Black Sea) and Ghilan (on the Caspian Sea)."

He also comments that they were evidently used for winter provision by the Lake dwellers of Parma,

Savoy, Lombardy, and Switzerland before they pos-
sessed metal, in the Stone Age. There is certainly
proof that they have been grown since prehistoric
times and for this reason I feel that probably
Sappho's Apple is at least a derivation of *M. pumila*,
the ancestor of modern varieties. We do not how-
ever possess many historical accounts of plants here
at Wisley and if you required more detailed infor-
mation it would be better to write to the British
Museum, who may be able to help you further.*

Some translators favor the *pomegranate*; which is not
impossible.

3. The apple as sacred to Aphrodite was a recognized
love symbol, cf. Aristophanes, *Clouds* 997, Theocritus,
6.6. with *Eclogues* 3.64: "Male me Galataea petit lasciva
puella." Further instances in Gow's note on Theocritus,
5.88.

4. See my note about "hyacinth" in poem 67.

### 93

Edm.152. Meter, probably hexameter.
From Cramer, *Inedita*.

1. The bride's reluctance to proceed with the marriage
was traditional sham. The bridesmaids pushed her from
behind into the bridal chamber and called out encour-
agement. See poem 94.

### 94

Edm.84. Meter, mainly choriambic.
From a seventh-century manuscript, conjecturally
restored.

*For this helpful letter I am indebted to Mr. C. D. Brickell, Bota-
nist, writing for the Director of the R.H.S. Gardens at Wisley at
Ripley in Surrey.

## 95

Edm.47. Meter probably Sapphic. From a second-century A.D. papyrus. This was the last poem in Sappho's Book I, which contained 1320 lines. See Campbell No. 30. I have conflated Edmonds with Campbell.

1. The bridesmaids probably kept up their wedding songs till dawn, stamping their feet in time and clapping.

2. Haines says:

> The writing of these epithalamia, or bridal songs, for friends and clients in Lesbos and elsewhere was an important and probably lucrative part of Sappho's professional work.*

**96**

Not in Edmonds. Found in Himerius, *Orations* 1/20, perhaps in imitation of Sappho. Weigall says: "seems to be Sappho's."

1. Himerius, the rhetorician, writing about 300 A.D.:

> It is she [Sappho] who after the mock combats enters the bridal precincts, decorates the room, spreads the couch, marshals the maidens at the bridal chamber, brings Aphrodite in her car of Graces, and a bevy of Loves to play with her.†

2. The bride would find herself in a candlelit room, the floor spread with sweet bay and the freshly made bed strewn with flowers and wet with perfume. Here her companions left her, clustering outside the door to sing through the night. The bridegroom entered, urged on robustly by his troupe of young men. After locking the door "his first business was to unveil the bride and to eat a quince with her as a pledge of future sweetness of speech."‡

*Haines 150
†*Orations*, 1/4 f.
‡Weigall 204

## 97

Edm.154. Meter, dactylic tetrameter.
From Hephaestion, *Handbook of Meter*.

1. The groom's friend, the θυρωρός, stands guard outside the door, which the bridesmaids attempt to force in order to rescue the bride. Meanwhile, the young men outside bang and kick, shouting their encouragement through the keyhole.

2. Demetrius, *On Style*:

> Sappho uses another style to make fun of the (supposedly) boorish bridegroom and the man who guards the wedding-room door. It is a very commonplace style and more like prose than poetry. In fact, these particular poems are better spoken than sung. They could hardly be adapted for the dance or the lyre, unless in a kind of dance dialogue.

Edm.159. Perhaps hexameter.
From Apollonius, *Conjunctions*.

Edm.155. Meter, choriambic plus iambic.
From Hephaestion, *Handbook of Meter*.

1. While the bridesmaids sing and the young men make a din (perhaps also sing, answering the girls) the marriage is consummated.

> It was only when the bridegroom came to the door and announced that all was as it should be that the people outside took their departure, though the bridesmaids grouped themselves near and continued to sing for the greater part of the night.*

Edm.128. Meter, doubtful.
From *Treatise on Etymology*: on the word δαύω"to sleep."

Edm.160 and 162. Meter, Aeolic.
From Hephaestion, *Handbook of Meter* and from Servius (c.390 A.D.) on Virgil. Referred to also by Pollux and Julian.

Edm.141a. Meter, dactylic.
From *Treatise on Etymology*.

Edm.164. Meter, choriambic.
Demetrius, *On Style*.

Edm.65. Meter, 14-syllable.
From a third-century papyrus: Oxy.Pap.1232/1.

1. And so the marriage night ends. The bride and groom are left in peace to greet each other over the morning cup. Later in the day they will receive the congratulations of their friends. The following night, to give his bride the chance of a complete rest, the groom sleeps in the house of his father-in-law and does not return to her till the third night—after more celebrations and another dinner party.

## 105

Edm.18. Meter, Sapphic.
From *Treatise of Etymology*.

*Weigall 204

1. Haines, Hill, and others join together the fragments of Edm. 17 and 18 and read ἄνεμοι for ἄνοαι:

. . . the drip of my pain—may driving winds bear it away with my sorrows.

**106**

Edm.121. Meter, Alcaic.
From Maximus of Tyre, *Dissertations:*

And what his rivals Prodicus and Georgias and Thrasymachus were to Socrates, that were Gorgo and Andromeda to Sappho. Sometimes she scolds them, sometimes she trips them up in argument, using exactly the irony Socrates uses. For instance, Socrates says: "A very good day to Master Ion," and Sappho . . .

1. Some read Πολλυανάκτιδα as a proper name:

A very good day to you, daughter of Pollyanax!

2. It is generally held that Andromeda was the mistress of a rival school of music and poetry at Mytilene and that Gorgo—a discarded friend of Sappho's—was one of the teachers. See poem 109. Since Andromeda could hardly boast of aristocratic lineage, it is clear that Sappho is here being sarcastic (if *she* is meant—but the reference could equally be to Gorgo.)

**107**

Edm.55. Meter, dactylic.
From Aldus, *Cornucopia* quoted by Choeroboscus (about 600 A.D.).

1. The Greek is:

. . . having had quite enough of Gorgo.

See note to poem 106.

Edm.74. Meter, choriambic (lesser Asclepiad).
From *Treatise on Etymology.*

Edm.81. Meter, Aeolic tetrameter.
From Hephaestion, *Handbook of Meter.*

1. Weigall writes:

> Atthis was a young girl; Sappho a woman in the
> later twenties, when the affair began. They were
> "bound together," says Suidas, "by an affection
> which was slanderously declared to be shameful";
> and it must have been chiefly on account of this
> slander, if slander it be, that Sappho's poems—so
> many of them addressed to Atthis—were burnt.*

Whatever the cause of Atthis' later desertion of Sappho
there is no record that the two were ever reconciled.
See also notes to poems 54 and 106, and poem 27 (if
indeed this refers to Atthis rather than to Anactoria),
and poem 116.

Edm.98. Meter, possibly choriambic.
From Athenaeus, *Doctors at Dinner:*

> . . . Sappho makes fun of Andromeda.

See note to poem 106.

Edm.49. Meter, 14-syllable.
From Apollonius, *Pronouns.*
He does not explicitly attribute this fragment to Sappho.

*Weigall 118

Edm.28. Only two words in the Greek.
From Maximus of Tyre, *Dissertations:*

> Diotima (in Plato's *Symposium*) says that Love flour-
> ishes when he is rich but dies when he is poor.
> Sappho put the two together and called him *bittersweet*
> (poem 109) and *giver of pain*. Socrates calls Love a
> wizard (sophistical), and Sappho a *weaver of tales*.

1. Pausanias (c.180 A.D.) says that:

> Sappho sang a lot of things about love that do not
> always agree.

Not in Edm. Meter, doubtful.
From Plutarch, *Symposium* 1/5/1.

Edm.90. Meter, unclassified.
From Aristides, *Orations* (in praise of Smyrna):

> . . . the glamour over the whole city, not as Sappho
> said, stunning the eyes, but magnifying it and crown-
> ing and watering it with buoyancy—not exactly "like
> a larkspur" but in a way that earth and sun have
> never before declared to man.

1. See note about ὑάκινθος "hyacinth" in poem 67.

Edm.21. Meter, Sapphic.
From the Scholiast on Apollonius of
Rhodes's *Argonautica:*

> (whether Jason's cloak was red or particolored?)

Edm.48. Meter, Sapphic-14-syllables.*
From Hephaestion, *Handbook of Meter*, on the Aeolic line.

Edm.69. Meter, choriambic (greater Asclepiad).
From Pollux (c.180 A.D.), *Vocabulary*.

1. Probably the description of a dream.

Edm.106. Meter, dactylic.
From Diogenian, *Centuries of Proverbs:*

> Said of those who will not take the sour with the sweet (or the thorns with the rose).

Not given in Edm., but D68 and LP 65. Meter, Ionic tetrameter of 16 syllables. From Oxy.Pap.1787 fragment 4.
The poem is so severely mutilated that even in these ten lines only 42 syllables out of 160 are extant. On these and something of a known context, I have based a reconstruction. It is interesting to compare this with Barnstone's translation of the Greek words as they stand:

> Andromeda
> forgot
>
> And I too
> blamed you,
>
> yet Sappho
> I loved you

*Reputedly the meter of the whole of Sappho's second book.

In Kypros I am Queen
and to you a power

as sun of fire
is a glory to all.

Even in Hades
I am with you.

Admirable in its own way though this is, the method
has its own pitfalls. It would be oversanguine to imag-
ine that by keeping strictly to the remains of Sappho's
words—without the possibility of reconstruction through
scholarship or the attempt to do so by historical
imagination—we necessarily come nearer to the sense
of the original. We might on occasion get even further
away. By analogy, for instance, compare the following
from *Antony and Cleopatra* (supposing that only these
words were extant and were linked syntactically):

She sat in
a burnished throne
the water was beaten
gold. The sails
[were] lovesick. The
silver tune of the flute
made the water follow
amorous [of]
her own person . . .

with the real passage:

The barge she sat in, like a burnished throne
Burned on the water; the poop was beaten gold,
Purple the sails and so perfumed, that
The winds were lovesick with them, the oars were silver
Which to the tune of flutes kept stroke, and made
The water which they beat to follow faster,
As amorous of their strokes. For her own person,
It beggar'd all description.

It would be easy to find more extreme examples still:

Not to be:
that is the question.
'Tis nobler to take arms
against a sea of troubles
and die.

Almost the reversal of what Hamlet said.

### 120

Edm.125. Meter, hendecasyllabic.
From Hephaestion, *Handbook of Meter*.
See also notes to poems 106, 109, 110.

1. Some translate:

Andromeda has got herself a pretty bargain.

### 121

Edm.119. Meter, Alcaeus' proposal is Sapphic with an
extra syllable at the beginning (which used to be called
"anacrusis"); Sappho's answer Alcaic.
The first line is from Hephaestion, 80, the rest from
Aristotle (writing about 330 B.C.) *Rhet.* 1/9.

1. Alcaeus, born about 600 B.C. (or probably earlier),
shared with Sappho not only the distinction of being
exiled for a time from Mytilene, but also preeminence
as a monodic lyric poet. His poems are concerned with
politics and war, love and wine. A typical theme is:

Drink, for one day you will die and there is no
return from Hades. Do not hope to be immortal.
Love the present moment while you are young.

He seems to have been an attractive if rather roister-
ous person. His sense of humor balked at nothing.
After a battle he once wrote home celebrating the fact
that he was safe and that his unconquerable shield had
had the honor of being captured and hung up by the
enemy before the blue gaze of Pallas Athene. In which

act of enlightened cowardice he had Archilochus as a precedent and Horace as an imitator.

2. Haines comments:

> In the lines attributed to Alcaeus . . . he uses a meter which is neither Alcaic nor Sapphic, but like both, being a Sapphic line with anacrusis and having one syllable more than the Alcaic, Sappho answers him in his own Alcaic stanza, intended no doubt by the compliment implied to soften the rebuke administered.*

3. Ivor Brown's comment:

> These are interesting verses to come from the "roaring boy" of the city in whom scruple about seduction was likely to be scanty. Some suppose that he wanted to marry her, but the words of his verse suggest that he wanted her "without string"; to ask for that, he felt ashamed.†

### 122

Edm.58. Meter, 14-syllable.
Quoted by Galen, writing about 160 A.D., *Exhortation to Learning:*

> And so it is better, since we know that the heyday of youth is like the flowers of spring and its pleasures fleeting, to agree with the Lady of Lesbos and say . . .

He adds that Solon said much the same thing. Compare Ben Jonson:

> How near to good is what is fair!

### 123

Edm.120. Meter, a form of Alcaic.
From Athenaeus, *Doctors at Dinner* (on lover's eyes):

*Haines 210
†Ivor Brown 116

To a man exceedingly admired for his appearance
and reckoned good-looking.

1. Weigall comments:

These words seem to have been written to a youth
who was shy of her, for they suggest a certain
condescension on her part; and one imagines her,
thus, greatly attracted by the handsome appearance
of this young man with the beautiful eyes, who,
either because of his youth or his humble social
standing, had bowed himself before so famous a
lady. Perhaps it was this selfsame personage who,
having been led on by her and allowed to become
intimate with her, lost his head and asked her to
marry him, thus evoking that sad cry from her: "I
am too old."* (poem 124)

### 124

Edm.99. Meter, Glyconic.
From Stobaeus, *Anthology*: on the advisability in mar-
riage of taking into account the ages of the parties.

1. It is sometimes supposed that Sappho is here ad-
dressing Alcaeus, but as far as we can tell Alcaeus was
older than Sappho. (Otherwise there is evidence that
might indicate that he was in love with her till the day
of her death.)

2. Weigall suggests that she may be addressing the
youth Phaon, for unrequited love of whom she is
supposed to have leapt to her death from the Leucadian
cliff. Weigall is almost the only modern scholar who
attempts to substantiate this tradition.

### 125

Edm.136. Meter, dactylic. This is a refrain.
From Marius Plotius, *Meter*. I have preserved the me-
ter in the English.

*Weigall 286

---

**1.** Adonis lived four months of the year with Aphrodite, four with Persephone, and four alone.

**2.** Haines and others read: ϝέσπετ' γμήναιον, which would mean: "Sing out the wedding song: Ah for Adonis!"

### 126

Edm.100. Meter, choriambic.
From the Scholiast on Pindar:

> Wealth bedecked with virtue makes possible all manner of things.

**1.** Sappho herself was undoubtedly a rich woman. Even if we did not know this from the fact that she married "a very rich business man,"* the internal evidence of her poems is enough to show that she was surrounded by all the appurtenances of refinement, even luxury. So too her exile, her travels, her social standing in Lesbos.

### 127

Edm.110. Not accepted by Page as Sappho's.
From the Scholiast on Pindar, corroborated by Pausanias. Edmonds has constructed the verses out of an adaptation of the Scholiast's citation.

**1.** Pausanias:

> The poetess of Lesbos is witness that gold is not tarnished by rust.

### 128

Edm.71. Meter, choriambic (greater Asclepiad).
From Stobaeus, *Anthology* (on Folly):

> Sappho, to a woman of no eduction.

*Suidas or—more correctly—the *Suda*. What it says is that he was rich, and that he came from or possibly traded from Andros.

Plutarch mentions the occasion twice: once as written to a rich woman and again when he says that the crown of roses was assigned to the Muses, remembering that Sappho had said the same words to an uncultured woman.

1. Weigall suggests that these harsh words were for Sappho's bête noire, Andromeda.

2. "Roses of Pieria" is of course a metaphor for poetry, Pieria, at the foot of Mount Olympus, being one of the traditional homes of the Muses.

## 129

Not included by Edmonds. Meter, Sapphic-14-syllables. From Stobaeus, *Anthology* 26 (Bergk 32$^n$).

Λαθα πίερισι στυγέρα και ἀνάρσιος

## 130

Edm.116. Meter, Saphic-16-syllables.
From Hephaestion, *Handbook of Meter*.

1. Haines and others read ἔιραννα (Eiranna, a girl's name) instead of φιρην α (Peace).

## 131

Edm.140. Meter, hexameter.
From Gellius, *Attic Nights*, on Niobe's children:

For Homer says she had six of either sex, Euripides seven, Sappho nine, and Bacchylides and Pindar ten.

1. Probably spoken in sarcasm. When Niobe boasted that she had more children than Leto, Leto's children— Apollo and Artemis—killed Niobe's children.

## 132

Edm.51. Meter, 14-syllable.
From Herodian, *Words Without Parallel*—not explicitly ascribed to Sappho.

Some read ἄλλαν μοι instead of ἀλλ' ἂν μὴ:

Go and boast to someone else about your ring.

### 133

Not given in Edmonds. Text from Page. Meter, predominantly Glyconic.
From a third-century papyrus, one of the most recent to be published by the Egypt Exploration Society. The number of stanzas is uncertain. The last stanzas are particularly sketchy and I have telescoped them together to get sense. (They may not even belong to the same poem.)

1. It appears that Sappho is in exile. One of the Cleanactidae—probably the tyrant Myrsilus—is in power. The shops of Mytilene are inaccessible to Sappho, who thinks wistfully of her remnants of finery: memorials to happier days. According to a scholia, she and other recalcitrant citizens had, by order, taken up residence in the town of Pyrrha: a town in the center of Lesbos, overlooking the inlet of Pyrrha. In another banishment (it is difficult to determine whether before or after this) she went to live in Sicily.

2. Sardis in Lydia was a center of feminine fashion.

### 134

Edm.36. Meter, Sapphic.
From a third-century papyrus. My text is compiled from Edmonds, Page, and Haines.

1. Edmonds thinks the poem may have been in the form of a letter handed to Charaxus on his return from Egypt, asking for a reconciliation. He was the eldest of Sappho's three brothers, all of whom were probably junior to her. Her favorite appears to have been Larichus, the youngest.

2. The poem has five stanzas, the last of which—except for a few words—is missing. I find Edmonds's recon-

struction of it a little too coarse-grained for Sappho (though she certainly had a temper) and have left it out:

and as for thee (Doricha), thou black and baleful she-dog, thou mayst set that evil snout to the ground and go a-hunting other prey.

3. Charaxus was at the time engaged in shipping wine from Lesbos to the Greek colony of Naucratis in Egypt. There he became infatuated with the beauty of Rhodopis —Rosycheeks—a famous courtesan and slave whose real name was Doricha. He bought her freedom at a great price and Sappho was shocked: perhaps not so much by the fact as by the extravagance of the liaison. After his return to Mytilene (or perhaps before) he expressed annoyance at his sister's interference and at her spreading the tale of his indiscretions. She seems then to have rounded on him with a poem which reduced him to ridicule. This we do not have (unless poem 138 is the last stanza of it).

4. Weigall supposes Doricha-Rhodopis to have been in her late twenties about this time (c.566 B.C.), basing his computation on the fact that she had once been the fellow slave of Aesop, who was probably born c.620 B.C. He thinks Charaxus was about forty-four and Sappho herself forty-six. Charaxus

is described as a refined, elegant personage, a man of taste and culture, who made a large fortune in the wine trade, but was sufficiently hardy and enterprising to conduct his own business and to come himself each year to Egypt with his fleet of wine laden ships.*

5. Athenaeus, *Doctors at Dinner*, writes: "The following epigram on Doricha was composed by Poseidippus, who often refers to her in his *Aesopeia.*"

*Weigall 239.

---

Doricha, only your bones now
Are decked by the rope of your hair
So soft and long
And that mantle breathing myrrh
You drew round Charaxus, fair—
Folding his flesh to yours
Till the time of the morning cup.
And now the white speaking pages
Of the love song of Sappho abide,
Abiding forever,
And your name is blessed and kept
By Naucratis as hers
So long as a ship from the sea
Goes sailing along
The sandy sides of the Nile.

See Also Notes 3 and 4 to Poem 138.

### 135

Edm.35. Meter, Sapphic.
From a third-century papyrus and a seventh-century manuscript.

1. Edmonds and others take this as probably a letter to the erring Charaxus. It is difficult to say what its order is in the series of Sappho's representations to her brother.

2. Of the four stanzas, the first is lost except for the last word, and the last so mutilated that what is given here is only conjecturally restored. (See notes on poem 134.)

### 136

Edm.70. Meter, choriambic.
Cited by Priscian (writing in the fifth century A.D.), *Grammar*.

### 137

Not in Edmonds. Meter, fragmentary.
Quoted by Athenaeus, *Doctors at Dinner*.

—πολλὰ δ’ ἀναρίθμα
ποτήρια καλαἶφις

## 138

Edm.37. Meter, Sapphic.
From a second-century papyrus: Oxy.Pap. 7. I have
compiled my text from Edmonds, Page, and Haines.

1. Of the three stanzas only this and fragments of the
others survive.

2. The poem appears to be another derisory letter
from Sappho to her brother Charaxus on the Rhodopis
affair (Sappho calls her by her real name, Doricha).
The sense of the letter is taunting, pretending to re-
peat the gossip going the rounds in Naucratis and
Mytilene: "Doricha's made a good swap of bedmates,
hasn't she!"

3. Herodotus, writing about 450 B.C., says:

> Rhodopis was in her heyday during the reign of
> Amasis. . . . She was Thracian by birth, slave to
> Iadmon the son of Hephaestopolis, and fellow slave
> of Aesop the fable writer. . . . Rhodopis arrived in
> Egypt under the conduct of Xanthes the Samian.
> She came to ply her trade, but was redeemed at a
> high price by a man from Mytilene—Charaxus, son
> of Scamandronymus and brother of Sappho the po-
> etess. Rhodopis, thus liberated, remained in Egypt;
> and such were her charms that she made a great
> fortune. . . .*

Charaxus actually married her.

4. Weigall writes:

> The end of the story is not known. It may be that
> Doricha failed to hold his love, or he to retain hers:
> at any rate, we read that she resumed her career as
> a courtesan and in so doing accumulated vast wealth.

*Herodotus ii/134 f.

Glamorous tales of her beauty and profligacy gathered around her, and centuries after her day she was remembered as a brilliant figure, the heroine of many legends.*

See notes to poem 134.

## 139

Edm.92.
Adapted from a letter of Eustathius' in *Opuscula*.

1. See notes to poems 134 and 138.

## 140

Edm.15. Meter, possibly Sapphic.
From a second-century papyrus: Oxy.Pap.1231.16.11–12.

## 141

Edm.137. Meter, dactylic tetrameter split into dimeters of five syllables.
From Plutarch, *On Restraining Anger*.

## 142

Edm.78. Meter, probably choriambic.
From the Scholiast on Apollonius of Rhodes's *Argonautica*.

1. This looks like one of Sappho's proverbs. The phrase she uses can mean either a heap of small stones or the pebbles on the beach. The first could denote the little piled-up mounds used to designate sacred precincts and her phrase would then mean: Don't meddle with sacred things; the second, *as* I have translated it, with the connotation: Let sleeping dogs lie.

*Weigall 243

Edm.11. Meter, Sapphic.
Adapted from a citation by Aristides, *On the Extemporized Addition.*

Edm.76 and 77. Meter, choriambic.
The two fragments, not necessarily from the same poem, are quoted by Dio Chrysostom, writing about 100 A.D., in his *Discourses.* His comment is: "Said with perfect beauty."

1. ἀμμέων strictly "us" (shall remember *us*) but here as elsewhere in Sappho probably of singular intent.

Edm.43. Meter, Sapphic.
From a second-century papyrus: Oxy.Pap.1231/13.
Emended and almost entirely reconstructed by Edmonds.

Edm.114. Meter, Ionic.
From Hephaestion, *Handbook of Meter.* He does not say these lines are Sappho's.

Edm.112. Meter, form of choriambic.
From Hephaestion, *Handbook of Meter.*

Edm.84A. Meter, uncertain.
Conjecturally restored from a citation by Libanius in *Orations,* where he seems to be referring to the story of Zeus's night with Alcmena when Heracles was conceived. Sappho's words, however, may well come from one of her lost bridal songs.

Edm.34. Meter, probably Sapphic.
From *Berliner Klassikertexte* 5 P 5006.
The fragment has been torn in half, leaving only the
last few words of each line. I translate them as they
stand, without any attempt at reconstruction.

Edm.82. Meter, hendecasyllabic.
From a seventh-century manuscript. Very tentatively
restored by Edmonds: many even of the few extant
words and letters in the MS. are only doubtfully legible.

1. Sappho apparently is recalling the scene described
in a letter Atthis once sent to her. Weigall imagines
the scene:

> It seems that Sappho had taken her daughter Cleïs
> and some of the girls, including Atthis, to stay
> during the hot summer months in the cool wooded
> uplands, perhaps on the slopes of the Lesbian Olym-
> pus; but in the autumn . . . her young companions
> were tired of their rustic life and were eager to get
> back to Mytilene. At last one day she promised to
> take them home on the morrow; but at mid-morning
> she was still in bed, and Atthis, impatient to be off,
> wrote her a letter which, I suppose, was to be sent
> in to her by a servant and which Sappho afterwards
> put into verse.*

2. Weigall's account does not easily accord with
Sappho's phrase "among us again." It is more likely
that Sappho was by herself in the hills and the rest of
the girls in Mytilene. Possibly (as Edmonds suggests)
this was the day of her return to Mytilene after her first
exile in the town of Pyrrha in the center of the island.

3. "A grandlier breakfast": literally "sweeter." The
ordinary Greek breakfast on the mainland was bread
dipped in wine.

*Weigall

Edm.113A. Meter, Anacreontic and Ionic.
From a papyrus of about 100 A.D. The readings are various.

1. Weigall, plausibly, but without secure foundation, comments:

> She was bitterly conscious of her years, and the slow process of the departure of her charms was watched by her in her mirror with increasing despair. There were still left to her, however, her personal magnetism, her grace, her graciousness, her elegance, her wit, and her brains; and these qualities, together with her fame and her wealth, evidently retained for her her social leadership in Mytilene; and filled her house with her friends and admirers.*

See also poems 152, 158, and possibly 155.

### *152*

Edm.42. Meter, Sapphic.
From a second-century papyrus: Oxy.Pap.1231/10.
Restored, almost in its entirety, by Edmonds. Hill takes τότ' ὄυ instead of τάχ' ὄυ and translated (without justification):

> . . . then of course I would be only too delighted to come, *with trembling footsteps* . . .

### *153*

Edm.103. Meter, choriambic.
From Hephaestion, *Handbook of Meter*.

### *154*

Edm.135. Meter, irregular Ionic or Aeolic.
From Hephaestion, *Handbook of Meter*.

*Weigall 284

---

1. Haines comments:

> Probably based on a folk song such as is found in
> many languages, e.g., in ours:
> "Oh mother put the wheel away
> I cannot sing tonight."†

2. Some read βραδίναν instead of βραδίνω: broken by
"*soft* Aphrodite's spell."

### 155

Edm.122. Meter, Ionic a minore.
From Hephaestion, *Handbook of Meter*.

1. Of the two daughters of Pandion who were changed
into birds, Procne is usually said to be the swallow and
Philomela the nightingale. The swallow for Sappho
suggests not only spring but love and passion: (Tereus,
Procne's husband, ravished her sister).

### 156

Edm.131. Meter, trochaic.
From the Scholiast on the *Plutus* of Aristophanes, to
show the meaning of the word ἡμιτύβιον:

> equivalent to "sudarium," a half-worn piece of linen
> like a dishcloth; compare Sappho . . .

In fact a "napkin."

### 157

Edm. 134. Meter, uncertain: ⏑⎯⏑⎯ ⎯⏑⏑⎯⏑⏑⎯, but at
least dactylic in effect.
From Aristotle, *Nicomachean Ethics*: "But love is a
wily thing, as they say of Aphrodite."

†Haines 118

It is not certain that Sappho is speaking of herself, since (in the Greek) the subject of the sentence is missing.

## 158

Edm.Appendix 118A. Meter, Sapphic-16-syllables. From a third-century papyrus: Oxy.Pap.1787/3/3.

1. So much of this fragment has been restored by conjecture (Edmonds) that I have adapted rather than translated the reconstituted Greek text, except for lines 16 to 27 in which I have followed the next text as given by Campbell. My old version, based on Edmonds's text, ran as follows:

Certain as rosy-armed Morning
Gives way to the night
Spread over with stars to the end of the earth—
So Death follows after and catches
Everything living.
He would not give back
Orpheus his darling wife.
And every woman who dies
He keeps in his thrall in the dark
Though he seems for a little to let her
Follow her spouse,
Piping and singing.
But for me etc. . . .

## 159

Edm.91. Meter, choriambic, lesser Asclepiad (if our restoration is correct).
From Aristotle, *Rhetoric.*

## 160

Edm.14. Meter, Sapphic.
From Apollonius, *Pronouns.*

Edm.50. Meter, Aeolic dactylic pentameter.
From Apollonius, *Pronouns*.

**162**

Edm.143. Meter, elegiac.*
From *Palatine Anthology*. The ascription to Sappho is
doubtful: the note in the MS. says: "Not in Michael's
copy, so I do not know its origin."

1. The inscription on the base of the statue is to a
nameless baby girl whose mother, a priestess of Artemis,
dedicated her to that goddess as a thank offering.

2. Haines and others read:   παῖδες, ἄφωνος . . . "Chil-
dren, though dumb, etc."

3. "Aethopia" in the Greek text is the goddess Artemis.
The meaning of the word literally is "burnt-face."

**163**

Edm.144. Meter, elegiac.
From the *Palatine Anthology*. Haines and others be-
lieve the ascription to Sappho doubtful.

1. Haines notes:

> Nothing is known of Timas as a friend of Sappho's
> unless we accept Edmonds's emendation of frag-
> ment (44) where he introduces the name of Timas
> (relying probably on *this* fragment). See *Proceed-
> ings of the Classical Association* 1921.†

See also *Glossary* of Hesychius, where there is a
reference to Timadia ("Little Timas") in a quotation

*The elegiac is said to have been invented for use with the flute, but
these words were an inscription for a monument and are unlikely
ever to have been sung.
†Haines 176

without context. Donald Lucas, writing to me from Cambridge, comments: "That ἀπυφθιμένας could mean 'die a long way from home' is wildly unlikely, and would not have been suggested but for the unjustified intrusion of Timas into Edm. fragment 87."

2. Weigall writes:

> From this epitaph it is perhaps to be gathered that the girl died in Sappho's house at Mytilene and that her ashes were sent to Phokaea for interment.*

It appears then that Timas was an Ionian from Phocaea, the northernmost city of the Ionian Confederacy.

3. Another possible translation of the first three words is:

> This dust is poor little Timas.

### 164

Edm. *Lyra Graeca,* III, p.438 (1940). Meter, perhaps Aeolic dactylic pentameter.
From the Scholiast of Sophocles' *Electra.* Edmonds ascribes it to Sappho or Alcaeus.

### 165

Edm.145. Meter, elegiac.
From the *Palatine Anthology.* Haines and others doubt the ascription to Sappho. I think that this doubt, from internal evidence at least, is ill-founded. . . . (Shall some New Zealander one day, finding in the ashes of London *Old Possum's Book of Cats,* say: "No one can suppose that this is by T. S. Eliot!"? Which words Haines uses of Sappho.)

*Weigall 274

Not in Edm. but in LP Incert. and T p.16. It is from the large collection of papyruses at Vienna, R. Rainer 29.777a. (Rainer was the archduke who gave his name to the collection.) Meter, Sapphic.

There are merely three lines in the Greek, and even these contain barely half their words. The problem of translation is exactly that posed by 119, 149, 66, and all those trantalizing fragments where there is not enough left to reconstruct the Greek but enough to make sense in English. Of which sense one must be particularly beware, as I point out in poem 119. Here, for instance, the subject of τελέσθην ("was brought to pass") is missing, and we can only guess at it. Lobel and Page give no warrant even for τελέσθην.

## 167

Edm.Appendix: 50A. Meter, Sapphic-14-syllables.
From a third-century papyrus: Oxy.Pap.1356/4a/114; in which Philo (the Jewish philosopher, first century A.D.), on the subject of punishment, says the penitent "gives way to the good advice of the poetess Sappho when she says . . ."

## 168

Edm.85. Meter, Aeolic (Glyconic with extra dactyl). From the reverse of the manuscript of fragment 148. More than half restored by Edmonds.

1. Edmonds omits the fragmentary opening:

$$. . . \mathring{η}ρ' \; ἀ\,[ . . .$$
$$δῆρα \; το\,[ . . .$$

and translates: "It won't be long now . . ."

Meter, Sapphic-16-syllables. Oxy.Pap.XV/1787 fragment 4.
Not given in Edmonds. Denys Page 65. Only about a quarter of each line survives.

Edm.108. Meter, choriambic (lesser Asclepiad if we supply before the first line).
From Maximus of Tyre, *Dissertations* (on what was the nature of Socrates' love affairs):

> Socrates scolds his wife Xanthippe for weeping when he is about to die, and so does Sappho scold her daughter.

1. It is hard to reconcile this fragment with the story that Sappho leapt to her death for love of the youth, Phaon. Weigall, one of the few who believe the legend, writes:

> . . . her reference to Death . . . may perhaps have been inspired by a recent close approach to the dark portals of the dreaded underworld. . . . But the fact that these carefully turned lines were included amongst her poems rather suggests that they were not composed when she was actually about to die but that they were written up, when her health was restored, as a poetical record of an injunction given by her at the time when she was ill.*

Edm.111. Meter, Aeolic or irregular Ionic ("the someter of languor").
From Hephaestion, *Handbook of Meter*.

---

*Weigall, Arthur, *Sappho of Lesbos: Her Life and Times.* London Thornton Butterworth, 1932.

---

1. Cox notes that with the "Hymn of Aphrodite" the "singularly beautiful fragment" was the first portion of the poems of Sappho printed in 1554.

2. Page will not bring himself to say that this fragment is by Sappho: the evidence is not against, but neither is it in favor of the attribution. A. W. Gomme takes him to task for this in *Journal of Hellenic Studies* LXXVI 1957, and Page makes a brief reply in *JHS* LXXVII 1958.

# GLOSSARY

ACHERON: One of the five rivers of the dead running
through Hades. The name means woe and was often
used synonymously for Hades itself. It was across
this river that grisly old Charon ferried the dead.
The other rivers were: Cocytus (wailing), Lethe (for-
getfulness), Phlegathon (fire), Styx (gloom): across
which Charon also ferried the souls of the dead.

ACHILLES: Son of Peleus and the sea nymph Thetis.
He was one of the chief commanders of the Greek
forces at Troy and the tragic hero of Homer's Iliad.
He slew Hector, champion of the Trojans, in single
combat and dragged his body in triumph around the
walls of Troy. He was in turn slain by Paris, one of
king Priam's fifty sons, and the cause of the Trojan
War.

ADONIS: A youth famous for his beauty, with whom
Aphrodite (Venus) fell in love. He was killed by a
wild boar while hunting and Aphrodite caused the
scarlet anemone (Anemone pavonina which grows
all over the Greek meadows and hillsides in spring)
to sprout from his blood. Once he was in the under-
world, Persephone fell in love with him and refused
to let him come back to earth, even though Aphrodite
had persuaded Zeus to allow this. It was eventually
arranged that he would spend part of the year in the
underworld (winter), and part of the year on earth
(spring and summer). His name became associated
with fertility, seed time, and harvest, and his feast
was celebrated by women all over Asia Minor and
Greece—beginning with lamentation and ending in
wild rejoicing. It is possible that according to Sappho

(No. 125) Adonis spent four months in Hades, four months on earth, and four months alone.

AEGEAN: The sea between Greece and Asia Minor.

AEOLIA: Named after Aeolus, god of winds. It came to comprise much of the western coast of Asia Minor and the Ionian islands of the Aegean, including of course Lesbos.

ALCAEUS: Born about 620 B.C. and therefore a contemporary of Sappho. He was her admirer and possibly her lover. His lyric poetry dealt mainly with love, drinking, battles, politics, and the sea. He wrote, like Sappho, in the Aeolian vernacular.

ANACTORIA: One of the young women in Sappho's entourage who seems to have left to get married to a soldier (probably), across the mainland of Asia Minor in the city of Sardis.

ANDROMACHE: The wife of Hector of Troy. She was a princess from the ancient city of Thebe in southern Asia Minor.

ANDROMEDA: One of Sappho's rivals on the island of Lesbos and perhaps also a poet. She seems to have attracted Atthis to her circle.

APHRODITE: The goddess of love and beauty (the Roman Venus). She was one of the twelve Olympians and born out of the ocean foam (aphros) near either the islands of Cyprus (at Paphos) or Cythera, and therefore often called Cypris or Cytherea. She resisted Zeus's advances, and he in retaliation married her off to his ugly crippled son Hephaestus (Vulcan). She had love affairs with many of the gods, especially Ares (Mars) and spawned some interesting children: Eros (Cupid) by Hermes (Mercury), Priapus (god of the phallus and fertility) by Dionysus (Bacchus), Phobus (god of fear and alarm) by Ares. She also had children by men: a son and a daughter by Adonis, Aeneas by Anchises of Troy. She hated and was hated by Zeus's wife Hera (Juno). She was Sappho's favorite god and ally.

APOLLO: The son of Leto (Latona) and Zeus, and the brother of Artemis (Diana). Also called Helios (the Sun), Hyperion, Phoebus. He was one of the twelve

Olympians and the god of light, order, music, medecine, healing, prophecy. He was the symbol of young male beauty.

ARES: (Mars), the god of war: son of Zeus and Hera (Juno) and one of the twelve Olympians.

ARTEMIS: (Diana), daughter of Leto and Zeus, sister of Apollo: the goddess of hunt and wild animals, also of the moon. Always a virgin.

ATHENAEUS: (170–230 A.D.) A Greek scholar living in Alexandria. He wrote a famous work in fifteen books called *Doctors at Dinner* in which learned men of his day talked about the men and women of antiquity.

ATREIDAI: The two sons of Atreus, king of Mycenae, Agamemnon and Menelaus, who became kings respectively of Argos and Sparta. It was Menelaus's wife Helen who went off with Paris and caused the Trojan war. Agamemnon was commander-in-chief of the Greek forces. He was later to be murdered by his wife Clytemnestra.

ATTHIS: A young woman in Sappho's group and one of her favorites. Like Anactoria, she left Sappho.

CHARAXUS: One of Sappho's three brothers, who traded in wine between the island of Lesbos and the Greek colony of Naucratis in Egypt. (See note on Nos. 134 & 135.)

CHIOS: An island in the Aegean south of Lesbos. It was famous for its wine and fruit; also for its harbor, which could accomodate eighty ships.

CLEANACTIDAE: The Cleanax Clan, a powerful family in Mytilene headed by the tyrant Myrsilus.

CLEÏS: Sappho's daughter, and possibly also the name of her mother.

COLOPHON: A town in Ionia (Asia Minor) famous for its cavalry, which was dispatched toward the end of a battle to finish off the enemy. From that we get the word *colophon*, which means an inscription or notice put at the end of a book marking its finish, or a publisher's emblem.

CRETE: A large island in the Mediterranean south of the Aegean sea, and a center of the worship of Aphrodite; also of the Minoan civilization, eponymous with King Minos, son of Zeus and Europa. Zeus in the form of a white bull charmed the Princess Europa while she was picking flowers with her maids in the meadows of Phoenicia. She eventually mounted his back and he headed for the sea, swimming off with her to Crete.

CYPRIS: Aphrodite.

CYPRUS: One of the largest islands of the Mediterranean, just west of southern Turkey. The favorite haunt of Aphrodite.

CYTHERA: An island in the Ionian Sea southwest of the Peloponnesus that competes with Cyprus as the land onto which Aphrodite stepped when she was born from the foam.

CYTHEREA: Aphrodite.

DIKA: The shortened form of Mnasidika, one of the girls in Sappho's circle.

DIONYSIUS OF HALICARNASSUS: A Greek historian of the first century, who left his native Halicarnassus in Asia Minor (now Bodrum) and came to Rome, where he wrote twenty books on the antiquities of Rome.

EOS: Goddess of Dawn. The Roman Aurora.

ERESUS: A town in Lesbos possibly the birthplace of Sappho (The birthplace also in the late fourth century B.C. of Theophrastus, Aristotle's most famous pupil: philosopher, botantist, and author of *Characters.*)

EROS: (Cupid), god of being in love: son of Aphrodite (Venus) and Hermes (Mercury). Also represented as the attendant of Aphrodite, a robust small boy armed with a bow and quiverful of arrows.

GELLO: The ghost of a woman who died young and preyed upon children. Possibly connected with the Semitic and Sumerian myths of Lilith and Gallu.

GONGYLA: One of Sappho's favorites.

GORGO: Perhaps a poet, and probably a rival of Sappho's.

GRACES: (Charites): three daughters of Zeus, Aglaia (Sparkle), Euphrosyne (Gaiety), and Thalia (Bloom). They were young, beautiful, and virgins, in constant attendance on Aphrodite. Their mission, in association with the Muses, was to generally sweeten the tenor of life. They were generally depicted naked and holding hands to show that kindness should be visible to all and friendship an unbroken chain.

GYARA: One of the Cyclades islands in the Aegean. Used later by the Romans for prisoners.

GYRINNO: (or Gyrinna): One of Sappho's circle.

HADES: (Pluto), son of Zeus and Rhea. One of the twelve Olympians. Married to Persephone (Proserpina) and king of the underworld. Hades also came to mean the netherworld itself.

HECATE: A moon goddess identified with Persephone in Hades, Artemis on earth, and Selene in the heavens. She presided over enchantments and magic.

HECTOR: Son of Priam and Hecuba, brother of Paris, and the most valiant of the Trojan heroes. Homer describes how he was challenged and slain outside the walls of Troy by Achilles.

HELEN OF TROY: The most beautiful woman in the world. Mythologically, the daughter of Zeus and Leda. She was married to Menelaus, king of Sparta, by whom she had one child, Hermione. Her elopement with the handsome Paris, prince of Troy, was the alleged cause of the Trojan War. After the defeat and destruction of Troy she was returned to Sparta.

HELLAS: The ancient Greek name for Greece.

HEPHAESTION: (fl.150 A.D.) Greek scholar of Alexandria, who wrote a book famous in antiquity called *Handbook of Meter*. He had been tutor to the Emperor Verus.

HEPHAESTUS: (Vulcan), the son of Zeus and Hera. God of fire, metalworking, and all crafts. He was deformed and lame, yet somehow managed to have as wife the beautiful Aphrodite, whom he caught in the act of her adultery with Ares. He threw a net over the guilty pair and reported them to the gods.

HERA: (Juno), wife and sister of Zeus. Queen of the gods and goddess of marriage and childbirth. She was vindictively jealous of all her husband's amours and persecuted his mistresses with a vengeance.

HERMES: (Mercury), son of Zeus and Maia (one of the seven minor immortals called Pleiades.) He ran messages for gods and mortals and conducted the souls of the dead to Hades. He became the god of travelers, trade, nimble speech, and thievery.

HERMIONE: Daughter of Menelaus and Helen. According to Sappho (No. 51) her beauty did not match her mother's.

HERMOGENES: (fl.c. 170 A.D.) Greek authority on rhetoric and style of ancient authors.

HERO: One of Sappho's young women.

HERODOTUS: (484–c.428 B.C.), "The father of history." The most important and enjoyable to read of all the early historians. He used his wide travels to illustrate his nine books of history with every kind of historical, geographical, and literary information.

HESIOD: His dates are uncertain, but lived probably toward the end of the eighth century B.C. With Homer he is one of the first poets of stature in the ancient world. Legend has it that he defeated Homer in a poetic contest. His *Works and Days* is a long poem describing and extolling the values of diligence on the farm. His *Theogeny* tells of the origins of the earth and the processions of the gods.

HESPERUS: (Vesper), the evening star. The brother of Atlas and either the father or the grandfather of the Hesperides: celebrated nymphs who guarded the golden apples (somewhere beyond the oceans), which Zeus gave to Hera on their wedding day.

HOMER: "The father of poetry," whose birthplace and even existence are disputed. Nevertheless, his two epics *The Iliad* and *The Odyssey* are not only the earliest works of great literature but they have never been surpassed. They became the "Bible" of the ancient Greeks who knew them by heart. Alexander the Great in all his campaigns kept a copy of *The Iliad* under his pillow. The conjectured date of his birth used to be about 900 B.C., but modern scholars now favor c. 750 B.C. Tradition has it that he was blind.

HORACE: (65–8 B.C.), one of the greatest of the Roman lyric poets and the son of a slave. His father managed to give him an excellent education, first in Rome and then at Athens. Later he came to the notice of Vergil, who befriended him and to whom he became only second in importance among the poets of the Augustan age. Like Vergil, he was patronized by Maecenas, Augustus's chief minister, who gave him a small farm in the Sabine hills not far from Rome. Horace took Sappho and Alcaeus for his models. His principal works are the *Satires*, the *Odes*, the *Epistles*, and the *Art of Poetry*.

IDAEUS: The herald who brought the message to Troy of Hector's betrothal to Andromache. The name was traditionally used for Trojan messengers and may have been derived from Ida, a famous mountain near Troy.

ILIAD: Homer's epic poem on the siege of Troy, written probably in the eighth century B.C. The wrath of Achilles is the pivotal point of the story, which ends with his slaying of Hector and dragging him around the walls of Troy. The poem covers about fifty days in the ninth year of the war.

ILIUM: The citadel of Troy, often used for Troy itself.

IMAGISM: The Imagists were a group of poets in England and America who turned the use of images (which all poets have used) into a system. They believed that the image should be clear, precise, true, and should take the place of statement. They also believed that rhythm rather than meter should be the vehicle of verse: (in other words, they wrote in free verse). Though poets soon found that these ideals were too restrictive, Imagism had an effect on poetry that has lasted to our own day.

IONIA: A region along the western coast of Asia Minor off the Sea of Ionia (which is part of the Aegean) named after Ion, son of Xuthus and Creusa and grandson of Helen. Not to be confused with another Ionia that is a group of seven islands in the Ionian

Sea, (part of the Mediterranean south of the Adriatic), lying between Sicily and Greece. This Ionia is named after Io, who swam this sea after she had been changed into a heifer maddened by gadflies.

IRANA: Possibly a member of Sappho's circle, but in the poem where the word occurs (No. 130) it can also mean peace.

JASON: The swashbuckling adventurer who sailed with the other Argonauts in quest of the Golden Fleece, which he finally obtained through the help of Medea, (a beautiful witch whom he married and who ten years later was to murder their two sons and also Creusa, the daughter of Creon king of Corinth. This is the subject of Euripides' great play *Medea*.)

LEDA: Wife of Tyndareus but seduced by Zeus in the form of a swan. There are many versions as to the outcome. One is that she laid two eggs from which hatched Castor and Pollux, and Helen and Clytemnestra. Another is that Nemesis (goddess of vengeance) laid an egg, which Leda found and hatched.

LESBOS: A large island in the northwestern Aegean off the coast of Asia Minor (Turkey). Famous for wine, women, and song, and the home of many poets including Sappho.

LETO: Mother of Apollo and Artemis. (The Roman Latona). Jeered at by Niobe for having only two children whereas she had ten sons and ten daughters, she appealed to her children. Apollo shot darts into all the boys, while Artemis dispatched all the girls except one.

LYDIA: A prosperous kingdom in western Asia Minor. Its capital, Sardis, was a center of art and culture. The Lydians are said to be the first to coin gold and silver.

MAXIMUS OF TYRE: (c. 125–185 A.D.) A Greek philosopher and rhetorician who lived in the reign of the emperor Marcus Aurelius, one of his pupils. There are forty-one of his disertations on moral and philosophical subjects.

MELEAGER: A Greek poet of the first century B.C. who was born at Tyre and died on the island of Cos. His

*Anthologia* (Garland of Flowers) was a collection of epigrams and short verses culled from forty-eight of the most esteemed writers of antiquity.

MENELAUS: One of the sons of Atreus and king of Sparta. The husband of Helen of Troy. After the war with Troy was over, he quarreled with his brother Agamemnon about whether they should leave for Greece or stay on in Troy. On the island of Lesbos they prayed for guidance to Zeus, Hera, and Dionysus, (No. 42).

MIDDLE AND NEW COMEDY: These are terms to distinguish the kind of comedy written in the fourth century B.C. onward by Menander and others from the comedies of Aristophanes in the generation before (Old Comedy). Concentrating on plots and types rather than on character and topical satire, Middle and New Comedy, through Menander and later the Roman Plautus, became the prototype of the modern comedy of manners perfected by Molière.

MNASIDICA: One of Sappho's group of women, who may have deserted her. Also called Dika.

MUSES: The nine Muses, daughters of Zeus and Mnemmosyne (Memory), lived on Mount Helicon, a sacred mountain in Boeotia. Their domain was all art and science. Calliope looked after epic poetry, Erato of lyric poetry, Clio—history, Euterpe—the flute, Melpomene—tragedy, Thalia—comedy, Polymnia—mime, Terpsichore—dance, Urania—astronomy. They were often depicted as holding hands and dancing in a chorus, symbolizing the fact that all the arts and sciences are related.

MYRSILUS: A member of the Cleanax clan, one of the powerful rival families of Lesbos. He rose to power in Mytilene early in the sixth century B.C. and may well have been responsible for Sappho's and Alcaeus's exile.

MYTILENE: The ancient and present capital of Lesbos.

NAUCRATIS: A Greco-Egyptian port in the Nile delta: a center of commerce between Greece and Egypt. It was here that Sappho's brother shipped wine from

Samos, and where he fell in love with Rhodopis, the famous Courtesan.

NEREIDS: The fifty daughters of Nereus: sea nymphs who lived with their father at the bottom of the sea.

OLYMPUS: The highest mountain in Greece (9,794 feet), located in Macedonia, and traditionally the home of the gods.

ORPHEUS: Son of Apollo and Calliope (the Muse of epic poetry). Such was his magical skill on the lyre that rivers stopped, mountains moved, and wild beasts were held still. He even charmed back from the underworld his beloved wife Eurydice, but glanced over his shoulder and lost her.

OVID: (43 B.C.–c.18 A.D.), one of the most important Roman poets of the Augustan age, who however offended the emperor in some way and was banished in mid-career for the rest of his life to the lonely Roman outpost of Tomis on the Black Sea. His *Art of Love, Metamorphoses*, and *Letters from the Black Sea* ensured his fame for all time.

PAEAN: Another name for Apollo as healer, derived from the hymn sung to him. In No. 82 fourth line from the end, Sappho uses the word Paean, which I have translated into the more familiar Apollo.

PALATINE ANTHOLOGY: An important source of Greek versified epigrams dating from the seventh century B.C. onward, compiled from earlier collections toward the middle of the tenth century B.C.

PANDION: King of Athens, the victim of a horror story if ever there was one. His daughter Procne married Tereus, king of Thrace. Tereus raped Procne's sister Philomela and cut out her tongue. She however got the news across by sending a tapestry to her sister in which she depicted her violation. The sisters revenged themselves on Tereus by killing the five-year-old son of Tereus and Procne and serving him up on a dish to his unsuspecting father. During the meal, they threw the boy's head onto the table. The gods changed Tereus into a hoopoe, Philomela into a nightingale, and Procne into a swallow. The name Philomela became a synonym for the nightingale.

What is curious is that in a nightingale's song two of its most characteristic sounds are those of: Teri Teri Teri Ity Ity ... Itys was the boy's name. (Pandion died of grief.)

PANORMUS: There were several cities by the name of Panormus, which means "fit for landing." One of them was near Ephesus in the Ionian province of Asia Minor. They all seem to have been centers of the worship of Aphrodite. The most famous Panormus (after Sappho's time) is the present Palermo in Sicily.

PAPHOS: A town on the southern coast of the island of Cyprus, which claimed the distinction of being near the spot where Aphrodite rose from the sea. It was therefore a center of her worship. Unmarried girls there are said to have been allowed a special dowry by the state for prostitution.

PARIS: Also called Alexander. Son of Priam and Hecuba of Troy, and brother of Hector. This lively and good-looking prince was brought up as a shepherd on Mount Ida (where he had been exposed as a baby), but when it was discovered who he was and he was accepted into the royal family, the troubles prophesied before his birth began. It was while visiting Sparta and while her husband Menelaus, the king, was away that he persuaded Helen "the most beautiful woman in the world" to elope with him. All Greece mustered to avenge this act, and thus began the Trojan War.

PARNASSUS: A high mountain overlooking Delphi in Greece, named after Parnassus the son of the sea god Poseidon (Neptune). The mountain was sacred to the Muses, Apollo, and Dionysus. It became synonymous with poetry.

PAUSANIAS: An orator, geographer, traveler, who wrote a history of Greece in ten books (in Ionic Greek) and settled in Rome about 170 A.D. where he lived to a great age. Pausanias had an insatiable curiosity and filled his history with precise accounts of the stories and superstitions of the peoples he came across in his travels.

PEITHO: The goddess of persuasion: the attendant and perhaps the daughter of Aphrodite.

PELAGON: There were several Pelagons (*pelagos* means the sea). Sappho's Pelagon in No. 165 was a simple, overworked fisherman.

PENTHILUS: A mythical hero and supposedly the ancestor of the powerful family of the Penthilidae in Mytilene during Sappho's lifetime. The Penthilus of her day was the father-in-law of Pittacus, master of Lesbos. The family was not favorable to Sappho.

PERSEPHONE: (Proserpina) Daughter of Zeus and Demeter (Ceres—goddess of crops). She was abducted by Hades, god of the underworld, and reigned there with him as queen during the winter but each spring returned to earth and to her mother, causing all nature to blossom.

PHAON: The young boatman who ferried people across from Mytilene to the mainland. His fabulous good looks turned the hearts of many women, among them possibly Sappho's. When he deserted her, according to this story, she committed suicide. The Roman poet Ovid in the second half of the first century B.C. wrote a famous account of the supposed love-match and Sappho's passion. Alexander Pope, in the eighteenth century, made an equally famous translation of it.

> If not from Phaon I must hope for ease
> Ah, let me seek it from the raging seas;
> To raging seas unpitied I'll remove;
> And either cases to live or cease to love.

PHOCAEA: A maritime city in the Ionian province of Asia Minor, southeast of Mytilene. In 539 B.C. it sent colonists to found the town of Massilia in the south of France (present-day Marseilles).

PIERIA: A spring in northern Greece on the slopes of Mount Olympus and the birthplace of the Muses. It became an epithet for poetry.

PINDAR: One of the most important lyric poets of Greece (518–436 B.C.) who came from Thebes. His odes celebrating athletic prowess at Olympia made him famous, and his hymns and paeans were sung in temples throughout Greece. His statue was erected in Thebes and when the city was destroyed by the Spartans, and then again later by Alexander the Great, Pindar's house was spared. He lived well into his eighties, it seems, though his dates are doubtful.

PITTACUS: (c. 650–c. 570 B.C.): one of the seven wise men of Greece. He led the Lesbians to victory against the Athenian colonists at Sigeum (near Troy) and slew their leader in single combat. Then for ten years he governed his fellow citizens with exemplary justice and enlightenment before laying aside the trappings of power and devoting himself to a peaceful life of literary pursuits.

PLACIA: A river and the surrounding plain near the holy city of Thebe near Mount Ida in the region of Troy.

PLATO: (c. 429–347 B.C.): With Aristotle, the greatest of the Greek philosophers. He taught Aristotle and was the student of Socrates. Almost all we know about Socrates comes from his famous dialogues, written in some of the finest prose ever penned by man. His influence as a philospher reaches down to our own day.

PLAUTUS: (c. 254–184 B.C.), Roman playwright who wrote some 130 comedies, of which twenty-two are extant. Though he took his plots from the Greek New Comedy, he made them his own and is the father of modern comedy.

PLEIDES: (or Pleiades): seven stars which were once the daughters of Atlas. They are visible from early May to early November and symbolize both the moist fecundity of spring and the fruitfulness of autumn.

PLUTARCH: (c. 45 A.D.–c. 120): Philosopher, essayist, biographer. We know more about antiquity from Plutarch than from any other ancient writer. He was born and retired in Chaeronea, a country town in Boeotia, spending some years in between in Rome, where he made use of the libraries to write his two most famous works: *Parallel Lives* and *Moral Essays (Moralia)*. No Greek writer is more instructive or entertaining. It was from North's translation of Plutarch that Shakespeare took the plot for his *Julius Caesar, Anthony and Cleopatra,* and other of his plays.

POLLUX: (fl. 186 A.D.): A Greek writer and philologist who produced a useful work called *Onomasticon* (Words and Names). He was born in Naucratis and taught at Athens.

PRAXILLA: Female poet of the early fifth century, who's home was the ancient and sophisticated city of Sicyon in the Peloponnese (southern Greece below the gulf of Corinth). Nothing is known of her work. Sicyonian shoes were once deemed a byword of male effeminacy.

PRAXINOA: One of Sappho's young companions.

PRIAM: King of Troy at the time of the Trojan War. Of his innumerable children the most famous are Hector, Paris, Troilus, Cassandra, and Creusa (who became the wife of Aeneas.) He was married to Hecuba, (powerfully portrayed in Euripides' *Hecuba* and *The Trojan Women.*)

PSAPPHO: (ψαπφω), as Sappho called herself in her native Aeolian Greek.

PYRRHA: A town in the center of Lesbos to which Sappho was once forced to retire.

RHODOPIS: (Rosy Cheeks): the courtesan lover of Charaxus, Sappho's brother. (See notes to Nos. 134, 135, 138.)

SARDIS: The capital of the prosperous kingdom of Lydia in Western Asia Minor. In 548 B.C. it became a province of the Persian empire under Cyrus. The Lydians enjoyed a high degree of civilization and were not only the first to mint gold and silver but the first to elevate athletics to a spectator sport.

SEMONIDES: Elegiac poet of the mid-seventh century B.C. (Not to be confused with Simonides of Amorgos —one of the Cyclades islands in the Aegean—who lived in the early sixth century B.C. and was a fierce misogynist.)

SIGEUM: A promontory near Troy and the site of many of the battles between Greeks and Trojans during the Trojan War. It was later colonized by the Athenians but disputed by the people of Lesbos between 620 and 570 B.C.

SOCRATES: (469–399 B.C.): the ugliest and most attractive of all the ancient Greeks. He lived in Athens, wrote no books, and drew around him a group of young men (including Plato) who were spellbound by his character and his discourse. We know him mostly through Plato's dialogues. He was put to death by the state for "corrupting the youth."

SOLON: (c. 640–c. 560 B.C.): poet, politician, and statesman. His wise lawmaking and his military sagacity put Athens well on her way to being the most important of the city-states in Hellas. He was one of the seven wise men of Greece.

SUIDAS: (or Suda): the name of a lexicon or encyclopedia compiled toward the end of the tenth century A.D. It is the source of much useful information about antiquity. Whether Suidas himself ever existed is doubtful.

STOBAEUS: A Greek anthologist of the early fifth century A.D. whose *Eclogue* and *Florilegium* preserve many precious relics of ancient literature.

THEBE: A city of Mysia in southern Asia Minor and the hometown of Hector's wife Andromache. It was sacked by Achilles during the Trojan War. This Thebe is not to be confused with the more famous Thebes in Greece, or the ancient religious and political capital of Upper Egypt on the Nile some four hundred and fifty miles south of Cairo.

THYONE: Another name for Semele, whom Zeus impregnated in a shower of gold, to produce the god Dionysus.

TIMAS: One of Sappho's companions, who came from Phocaea in Asia Minor and died young.

TITHONUS: The brother of Priam, king of Troy. Such was his beauty that Eos, goddess of dawn (Aurora), fell in love with him and obtained for him the gift of immortality, but the pair forgot to ask for eternal youth. He grew old, wrinkled, and bent, and chattered so much that Eos had him changed into a cicada, (also presumably immortal).

TROY: (Also called Ilion and Ilium): the subject of Homer and Vergil's great epics, the *Iliad* and the

*Aeneid.* For ten years the Greek armies besieged Troy, the capital and jewel of northern Asia Minor. The city was taken in the tenth year only by a trick: the ruse of the Wooden Horse.

ZEUS: The Father of the gods and the chief of the twelve Olympians.

# Bibliography

Barnard, Mary. *Sappho.* A new translation, foreword by Dudley Fitts. Berkeley and Los Angeles: University of California Press, 1958. A refreshing antidote to some of the old metrically padded versions. The last vestiges of fustian are removed. However, modern syllabic verse cannot possibly give an indication of Sappho's tight preoccupation with meter and sound.

Barnstone, Willis. *Lyrics in the Original Greek with Translations.* New York: Doubleday, Anchor Books, 1965. With its inclusion of the Greek text, printed *en face*, this book becomes indispensable for anyone interested in Sappho. Honest and scholarly.

Bergk, Theodor. *Sappho*: Poetae Lyrici Graeci. Lipsiae, 1867. Greek text with notes in Latin. Out of date now but one of the most important scholarly editions of the last century.

Bowra, C. M. *Greek Lyric Poetry.* Latest edition, Oxford: 1961. Many texts of poems, Greek and English, with excellent critical comment, information, and exegesis.

Brown, Ivor. *Dark Ladies.* London: Collins, 1957. A collection of essays on strong-minded women, including Sappho and Cleopatra. Perceptive and enjoyable.

Campbell, David A. *Greek Lyric.* Cambridge, Mass., Harvard University Press, and London, William Heinemann Ltd., 1982. This edition supercedes the former *Lyra Graeca* by J. M. Edmonds in the Loeb Classical Library. It contains the most scholarly text since that of Lobel and Page.

---

Carman, Bliss. *Sappho: One Hundred Lyrics*. Boston: L. C. Page & Co., 1904, and London: Chatto & Windus, 1907. Re-creations in the style of Sappho, weaving complete new poems round isolated fragments. Sensitive, imaginative, and surprisingly restrained for the period. Among all the adaptations and reinventions, my favorite.

Cox, Edwin Marion. *The Poems of Sappho*. London: Williams & Norgate, and New York: Charles Scribner's Sons, 1924. Historical and critical notes, translations (of various excellence and accuracy), and a full but rather out-of-date bibliography.

———. *Sappho and the Sapphic Metre in English*. London: Charles Whittingham, 1916. A useful compendium of the history of Sappho translations into English, and also of the attempts to reproduce the Sapphic stanza. Cox, however, does not discuss theory or express an opinion on the plain truth of the matter, which is that the Sapphic meter in English works for only very short stretches, and even then is not the aesthetic equivalent of the Greek.

———. *Sappho*. Manaton, Devon: The Boar's Head Press, 1932. The text arranged with translations, introduction, and notes. Woodcuts by Lettice Sandford.

Davenport, Guy. *Sappho: Poems and Fragments*. Ann Arbor, The University of Michigan Press, 1965. An exciting rendering of the Lobel and Page collection, with an introduction which is a model of intelligence and grace. Most of the newer fragments are cited: allowed to remain in their tantalizingly beautiful brokenness. Commenting on this translation in *The New York Review of Books* (March 3, 1966), Professor D. S. Carne-Ross writes: "Davenport has justifiably brought into his version the radiance that can surround Sappho's single words . . . and he is the only man who has re-created in English the kind of intense poetry that we find—that we half invent, of course—in the broken fragments. Where he fails is with the longer, with the great, and very great, poems."

---

Diehl, Ernst. *Anthologia Lyrica Graeca.* Leipzig: Teubner Press, 1936. An important standard text, though now superseded by Lobel and Page.

Edmonds, J. M. *Lyra Graeca*, Vol. I. Loeb Classical Library, London: William Heinemann, and Cambridge, Massachusetts: Harvard University Press, 1958 (latest edition). Full Greek text edited and reconstructed by Edmonds (and others), together with literal prose translations. Still the indispensable collection for giving a total impression of Sappho's range, mood, and technique. This is the text on which I based my original translation, corrected and supplemented, however, in this edition, by recourse to more recent collections.

———. *Sappho:* In the Added Light of the New Fragments, being a paper read before the Classical Society of Newnham College, 22 February 1912. London: Deighton Bell, 1912. One of the first scholarly reactions to the Oxyrhynchus finds.

———. *Sappho Revocata:* Being an emended text with an English translation, a life and glossary of Aeolic words, with two drawings by Vera Willoughby. London: Peter Davies, 1928. A handsome book. The translations are in archaic rhymed verse.

Green, Peter. *The Laughter Of Aphrodite.* New York: Doubleday, 1966. A novel of the confessional genre, in which Sappho moves through her own life in retrospect, toward the moment of final tragedy. It is a riveting story, at once radiant and devastating, in which a massive reading of the classical context, and a sharply detailed reconstruction, ingeniously assimilates all the known facts about Sappho and a host of fascinatingly conjectured new ones. It is a picture of Sappho that I personally—after translating her for two years—can believe in. The author wrote the novel on the island of Lesbos.

Groden, Susy Q. *The Poems of Sappho.* Indianapolis, The Library of Liberal Arts, 1966. A useful translation. The Introduction deals particularly well with Sappho's strengths and some of her supposed weaknesses.

Haines, C. R. *Sappho: The Poems and Fragments*. Greek text with an English translation, also 20 plates (comprising 43 illustrations). London: C. Routledge, and New York: E. P. Dutton, 1926. A useful book. The photographs of busts of Sappho, of effigies on coins and vases, etc., are particularly interesting.

Hill, Maurice. *The Poems of Sappho*. London and New York: Staples Press, 1953. Greek text with an English verse translation. Useful for sidelights on an alternative text. The verse however would be better off as prose.

Lefkowitz, Mary R, and Fant, Maureen B. *Women's Life in Greece and Rome*. London, Duckworth, 1988. A unique collection of texts from ancient sources, illustrating women's accomplishments, occupations, conversation in Greece and Rome from classical times to early Christianity.

Lloyd, John A. T. *Sappho: Life and Work*. London: Arthur L. Humphreys, 1910. Retains a certain value in that it supplies odd bits of information from wide reading of the classical background. It is interesting to watch Sappho-philes of fifty years ago marshaling arguments to establish Sappho's unimpeachable morality.

Lobel, Edgar. *Sappho: Σαπφους μέλη*. London: 1925. A great work of scholarship, the results of which were later brought up to date and incorporated into *Poetarum Lesbiorum Fragmenta*.

Lobel, Edgar *et al.*, eds. *Oxyrhychus Papyri*. London: Egypt Exploration Society, 1951. A monumental work of collection, deciphering, and publication of the Greek papyruses (including Sappho) unearthed early this century at Oxyrhynchus. Publications are released at intervals of several years.

Lobel, Edgar, and Page, Denys. *Poetarum Lesbiorum Fragmenta*. Consisting of the works of Sappho and Alcaeus, with fragments of other unknown authors. Oxford: Clarendon Press, 1955. The completest and most scholarly edition of the Greek text of Sappho to date (prior to David Campbell's edition of 1982) comprising every fragment and part of a fragment so far discovered and published.

Marx, Olga, and Morwitz, Ernst. *Poems of Alcman, Sappho, Ibycus:* Rendered from the Greek. New York: Alfred A. Knopf, 1945. (One of 950 copies designed and printed by Bruce Rogers.) An attractive volume with Greek and English text. An interesting attempt is made to render the Sapphic meters in English, proving once again that this never produces an aesthetic equivalent. The pace of the Greek is far quicker and the effect less "wordy."

O'Hara, John Meyers. *The Poems of Sappho.* An interpretive rendition into English. Portland, Maine: Smith & Sale, 1924. Largely invention, though sometimes metrically interesting. Separate lines of Sappho lumped together to make complete poems.

Page, Denys L. *Sappho and Alcaeus:* An Introduction to the Study of Ancient Lesbian Poetry. Oxford: Clarendon Press, 1955. Text of twelve poems, critically edited, with prose translations, exegesis, and notes, by the shrewdest modern authority on Sappho.

Patrick, Mary M. *Sappho and the Island of Lesbos.* London: Methuen, 1912 and 1927. The text gives a plausible picture of the probable background of Sappho: food, customs, clothes, contemporaries, etc. There are also photographs of Lesbos and Mytilene as they are today.

Quasimodo, Salvatore. *Lyrici Greci.* Milan: Biblioteca Moderna Mondadori, 1951. Selected poems in Greek, translated into Italian verse. It shows how the problem of translation is resolved by a modern Italian poet; and, incidentally, that Italian has far less of a formal problem to solve than English.

Riencourt, Amaury de. *Women and Power in History.* London, Honeyglen Publishing, 1983. A timeless survey of the struggle to achieve a balance between patriarchal and matriarchal dictates. The chapters on ancient Greece (The Intellectual Breakthrough) and the Italian ethos (Roman Matrons and World Empire) are especially enlightening.

Robinson, David M. *Sappho and Her Influence.* Our Debt to Greece and Rome, No. 2. London: George G. Harrap, 1925. Reviewed thus by J. M. Edmonds in the *Classical Review*, Vol. XXXIX, p. 104, 1925: "He has accumulated a mass of material—literary, biographical, archaeological—for which any future writer on Sappho will be in his debt. But there is a third ingredient of which his supply is short—critical judgment. And the resultant dish, to put it brutally, is too much like a bibliography to be a book."

Smyth, Herbert Weir. *Greek Melic Poets.* London: Macmillan, 1904. An edition of the lyric poets in selection with scholarly introduction and notes. An important work in its day, but in some ways necessarily out of date.

*The Songs of Sappho.* In English translation by many poets, decorated by Paul McPharlin. Mount Vernon, New York: Peter Pauper Press, 1942. A useful book in that it gives several of the well-known versions of each poem.

Stacpoole, Henry de Vere. *Sappho.* A new rendering. London: Hutchinson, 1920. Paraphrases rather than translations but often beautiful.

Thompson, Maurice. *The Sapphic Secret.* Atlantic Monthly, March 1894. Translations of many of the shorter fragments. He emphasizes "the amazing power of Greek words as words," and this is shown "in such a way that phrases like ripe fruit-clusters seem bursting with the rich juice of passionate meaning."

Treu, Max. *Sappho.* München, 1958. An important edition; it does for German scholarship what Lobel and Page do for English. An invaluable source.

Tunison, J. S. *The Sapphic Stanza.* Granville, Ohio: The University Press, 1896. A tentative study in Greek metrical, tonal, and dancing art.

Tutin, J. R. *Sappho, The Queen of Song.* London and Edinburgh: The Foulis Books, 1911. A collection of translations from the Greek of Sappho, arranged by J. R. Tutin, with illustrations from pictures from watercolors by Ernest H. R. Collings. Paraphrases of Georgian and pre-Georgian vintage together with somewhat pre-Raphaelite paintings.

Way, Arthur S. *Sappho and the Vigal of Venus.* London: Macmillan & Co., 1920. Though an accomplished scholar, one of the archpractitioners of turn-of-the-century translationese.

Weigall, Arthur. *Sappho of Lesbos: Her Life and Times*. London: Thornton Butterworth, 1932. Reconstruction of Sappho's life, based on historical imagination and the extant poems and fragments. Fascinating and plausible, but largely unproven.

Wharton, Henry Thorton. *Sappho*. Memoir, text, and selected renderings, and a literal translation. London: 1885, with several reprints. This was the standard edition in English until Smyth and Edmonds. Though necessarily incomplete now, it retains its charm. The bibliography lists translations into French, German, Spanish, and Italian: interesting but dated.

Williams, William Carlos. *Sappho*. A translation. Poems in Folio, Grabhorn Press, 1957. This is a translation of the single poem φάινεταί μοι κηνος (He is a god in my eyes that man, etc.) in modern syllabics and stress rhythm. This important modern poet is faithful to the text, but the result is better Williams than it is Sappho. The stresses fall too uncertainly in English to give any idea of the Greek tightness of form.

Σαπφοῦς Μέλη. Munich: Bremer Presse, 1922. Beautifully printed Greek texts on hand-rolled paper. For those who have any Greek this book is an object to possess, but probably impossible to come by.